Oxford AQA GCSE History

Migration, Empires and the People

c790–Present Day

AUTHORS

Aaron Wilkes

Kevin Newman

SERIES EDITOR

Aaron Wilkes

CONSULTANT

J. A. Cloake

OXFORD

UNIVERSITY PR

OXFORD
UNIVERSITY PRESS

Great Clarendon Street, Oxford, OX2 6DP, United Kingdom

Oxford University Press is a department of the University of Oxford.

It furthers the University's objective of excellence in research, scholarship, and education by publishing worldwide. Oxford is a registered trade mark of Oxford University Press in the UK and in certain other countries.

British Library Cataloguing in Publication Data

Data available

978-138-202307-8

Digital edition 978-138-202308-5

3 5 7 9 10 8 6 4

Paper used in the production of this book is a natural, recyclable product made from wood grown in sustainable forests.

The manufacturing process conforms to the environmental regulations of the country of origin.

Printed by CPI Group (UK) Ltd, Croydon CR0 4YY

Approval message from AQA

This textbook has been approved by AQA for use with our qualification. This means that we have checked that it broadly covers the specification and we are satisfied with the overall quality. Full details of our approval process can be found on our website.

We approve textbooks because we know how important it is for teachers and students to have the right resources to support their teaching and learning. However, thepublisher is ultimately responsible for the editorial control and quality of this book.

Please note that when teaching the AQA GCSE History course, you must refer to AQA's specification as your definitive source of information. While this book has been written to match the specification, it cannot provide complete coverage of every aspect of the course.

A wide range of other useful resources can be found on the relevant subject pages of our website: www.aqa.org.uk.

The publisher would like to thank Jon Cloake for his work on the first edition of the Student Book on which this second edition is based. The publisher would also like to thank Chris Edge, Ben Fuller (Holocaust Educational Trust) and David Rawlings for their contribution in the development of this book.

Contents

Migration, Empires and the People c790–Present Day

Introduction to the Oxford AQA GCSE History series

The Oxford AQA GCSE History series has been specially written by an expert team of teachers and historians with examining experience to match each part of your AQA course. The chapters which follow are laid out according to the content of the AQA specification. Written in an interesting and engaging style, each of the eye-catching double-pages is clearly organised to provide you with a logical route through the historical content.

There is a lively mix of visual **Sources** and **Interpretations** to enhance and challenge your learning and understanding of the history. Extensive use of photographs, diagrams, cartoons, charts and maps allows you to practise using a variety of sources as evidence.

The **Work** activities and **Practice Questions** have been written to help you check your understanding of the content, develop your skills as a historian, and help you prepare not just for GCSE examinations, but for any future studies. You can develop your knowledge and practise examination skills further through the interactive activities, history skills animations, practice questions, revision checklists and more on *Kerboodle**.

Britain: Migration, Empires and the People c790–Present Day

This book guides you through one of AQA's Thematic Studies, Britain: Migration, Empires and the People c790–Present Day. Thematic studies focus on key developments in the history of Britain over a long period of time. You will look at the importance of factors such as war, religion, government, economic resources, science and technology, ideas and the role of individuals, and how these factors impact upon society.

Understanding history requires not just knowledge, but also a good grasp of concepts such as causation, consequence and change. This book is designed to help you think historically, and features primary sources; these sources will help you think about how historians base their understanding on the careful evaluation of evidence from the past.

We hope you'll enjoy your study of Migration, Empires and the People –

Jon Cloake
Series Consultant

Aaron Wilkes
Series Editor

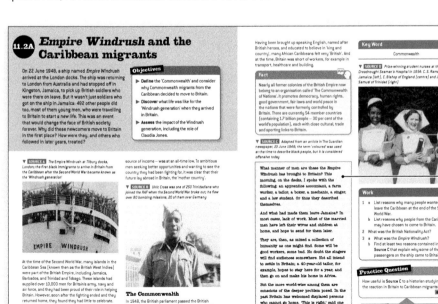

Sources provide opportunities for you to assess the usefulness of texts or images that are primary or contemporary to the period.

Practice Questions and Study Tips help familiarise you with new-style exam questions.

*Kerboodle is not approved by AQA.

How to use this book

Written for the new AQA specification, the features in this book include:

Objectives

At the beginning of the sections, you will find a list of learning objectives. These are based on the requirements of the course.

▼ SOURCE ▼ INTERPRETATION

Sources introduce you to material that is primary or contemporary to the period, and **Interpretations** provide you with various people's different perspectives on the past.

Practice Question

These are focused questions to help you practise your history skills, including evaluating sources and essay writing. They give you an idea of the types of questions you might get in an examination.

Study Tip

These are hints to highlight key parts of **Practice Questions** and will help you answer the questions.

Fact

Fascinating references, facts or anecdotes that will make you think and add to your knowledge and understanding.

Work

The activities and questions aim to develop your knowledge, understanding and key history skills. They are designed to be progressive in terms of difficulty, and to get you to think about the topic, become familiar with the history, and apply what you have learned.

Extension

This is an opportunity to challenge you to investigate the history more deeply through independent research and reflection.

Key Words

The important phrases and terms are highlighted and are also defined in the glossary. Learn what they mean — and how to spell and use them correctly.

Timeline

A short list of dates identifying key events to help you understand chronological developments.

Key Biography

Details of a key person to help you understand the individuals who have helped shape history.

Timeline

Britain: Migration, Empires and the People

This thematic study covers over 1000 years of the history that shaped much of what Britain is like today. You will get the chance to explore how the identity of the people of Britain has been created by their interactions with the wider world. You will have the opportunity to consider invasions and conquests and study the country's relationship with Europe and the wider world. You will examine the ebb and flow of people into and out of Britain, and will evaluate their motives and achievements. You will also consider the causes, impact and legacy of the British Empire upon the ruled and the ruling in the context of Britain's acquisition and retreat from its empire.

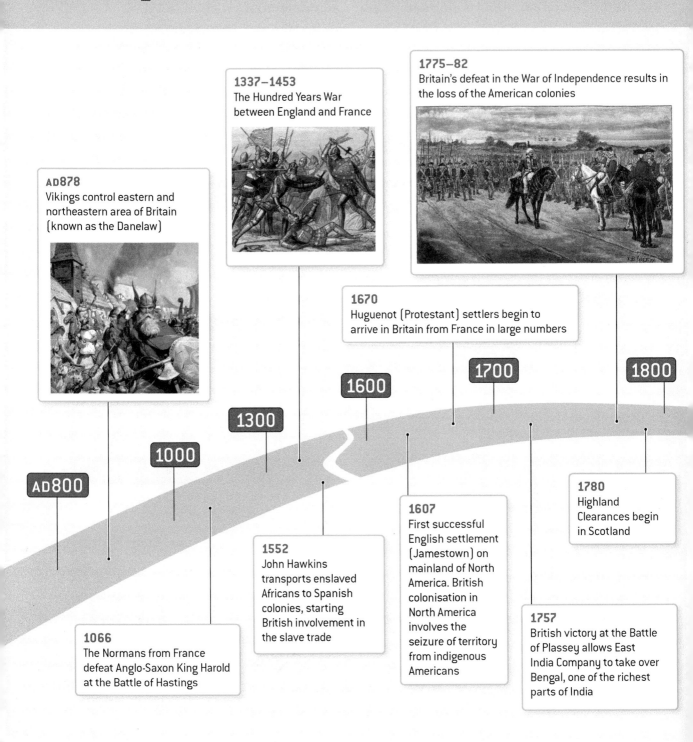

1775–82
Britain's defeat in the War of Independence results in the loss of the American colonies

1337–1453
The Hundred Years War between England and France

AD878
Vikings control eastern and northeastern area of Britain (known as the Danelaw)

1670
Huguenot (Protestant) settlers begin to arrive in Britain from France in large numbers

1800

1700

1600

1300

1000

AD800

1780
Highland Clearances begin in Scotland

1607
First successful English settlement (Jamestown) on mainland of North America. British colonisation in North America involves the seizure of territory from indigenous Americans

1552
John Hawkins transports enslaved Africans to Spanish colonies, starting British involvement in the slave trade

1757
British victory at the Battle of Plassey allows East India Company to take over Bengal, one of the richest parts of India

1066
The Normans from France defeat Anglo-Saxon King Harold at the Battle of Hastings

1948
Empire Windrush arrives in Britain, beginning a new period of migration from Caribbean countries

1881–1914
Scramble for Africa sees the invasion and colonisation of most of Africa by Britain and other European powers

1999
Twelve members of the EU agree to adopt the Euro as their currency, but Britain continues to use the Pound

1845–49
Irish potato famine sees mass starvation in Ireland and the emigration of around one million people

1973
Britain joins the European Union

1899–1902
The Second Boer War is fought between Dutch settlers (the Boers) and the British army

2000

1900

1950

1857–58
Indian Rebellion results in India coming under the formal control of the British government

1947
India gains independence from Britain

1982
The Falklands War between Britain and Argentina over the disputed Falkland Islands near South America takes place

1.1 Why did the Vikings invade Britain?

This topic focuses on the people who came to and left Britain, and the different **empires** Britain belonged to and built, from c790 to the present day. Different groups of people have been moving to Britain and settling for various reasons, and have made lasting contributions to British culture. Britain had also taken over land in other parts of the world: at one point in time, the British ruled over more land than any other country before or since. However, there have been times in Britain's history when it has been controlled by another, more powerful nation, and has been part of their empire. What was Britain like before the AD790s?

Objectives

▶ **Explore** the history of invaders and settlers in Britain.

▶ **Examine** how Britain came to be under Anglo-Saxon rule.

▶ **Explain** the reasons why the Vikings invaded Britain in the AD790s.

The first Britons

The timeline below charts the history of settlement in Britain up to the time this thematic study begins.

Fact

Historians sometimes add a 'c' before dates. This stands for 'circa', which means 'around' or 'approximately'.

Timeline

Before c4000BC:	c4000BC:	c500–43BC:
The first people who live in Britain are **immigrants**. They arrive from Europe around half a million years ago and are **hunter-gatherers**. They move around in small groups and learn skills such as lighting fires and making tools	Around 6000 years ago, farmers arrive from Europe, bringing seeds to grow crops and animals. They begin to clear some of Britain's thick woodland to create farms and build stone houses	About 2500 years ago, a new group of settlers begin arriving from central Europe. They are called the Beaker People after their beaker-shaped pottery cups; they also know how to make things out of metal. The next **tribes** to arrive and settle in Britain are Celts: they too farm the land and fight fiercely between themselves and with the people already settled here. Over many centuries, they merge with the original population

Fact

The Romans were the first people to use the name 'Britannia' for Britain. The name was based on the word 'Pretannia', which is what the Ancient Greeks called Britain: they thought a Celtic tribe called the 'Pretani' lived there. In fact, the Pretani tribe lived mainly in Ireland, but the name stuck, and later became 'Britannia', and then simply 'Britain'.

The strongest Anglo-Saxon tribal chiefs were known as Bretwalda or 'Ruler of Britain'. By AD800, most Anglo-Saxons had converted to Christianity, and merchants traded goods all over the country and into Europe, making some Anglo-Saxon kingdoms very wealthy.

From around AD400 onwards, Anglo-Saxons settled in villages next to their farmland. They set up a number of different kingdoms, led by lords and chieftains. The most powerful lords acted like local kings and fought one another to gain more land.

◀ **A** *Anglo-Saxon treasures like this war helmet were uncovered at the Sutton Hoo Saxon burial site in East Anglia, England*

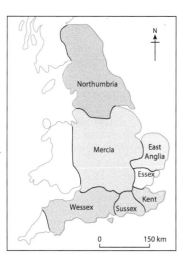

▶ **B** *A map of the Anglo-Saxon kingdoms, around AD700. The white areas in the south-west (Wales and Cornwall) were occupied by the original Celtic Britons. Over time, the area of Britain where the Anglo-Saxons settled became known as 'Angle-land', and later 'England'.*

Who were the Vikings and why did they attack?

In the mid-700s, the people of Scandinavia (Norway, Denmark and Sweden) began to explore, raid and eventually invade the countries around them. They sailed to Britain, Ireland, France, Spain and Italy. Others travelled by land, going as far as Israel, Greenland and probably America. They were known as **Vikings**, or Northmen, and began their raids on Britain around the AD790s.

Key Words

empire immigrant hunter-gatherer tribe Viking enslaved

The Vikings attacked Britain because they had traded goods with the Anglo-Saxons for many years, and knew of their wealth. The first recorded attack was on the monastery at Lindisfarne in Northumbria in AD793, and two years later they attacked the Isle of Iona in Scotland. To begin with, they attacked in the summer when the seas were calmer for their small ships. They raided villages and monasteries near the coast, and then sailed back with stolen gold and silver, cattle and even **enslaved** people. Later, they sailed up rivers and attacked further inland, and they sometimes stayed for long periods of time and built camps.

▼ **INTERPRETATION D**
A twentieth-century interpretation showing Vikings attacking the English; Vikings are often portrayed as wild, unsophisticated and bloodthirsty

AD43–401:

The Romans arrive from Italy and conquer most of the British tribes. The Romans stay and rule for over 400 years, and the country becomes part of the huge Roman Empire

AD401 onwards:

By AD401, the Romans in Britain are called back to Italy to defend their homeland from invasion. The British who have lived under Roman rule are left to fend for themselves, and soon new tribes invade. They come by boat from Denmark and northern Germany looking for a better climate and good farmland. These tribes are called Angles, Saxons and Jutes. They soon become known as Anglo-Saxons and, after fighting with the British tribes, capture most of Britain (except Cornwall, Wales and the far north)

▼ **C** *A map of the main Viking voyages*

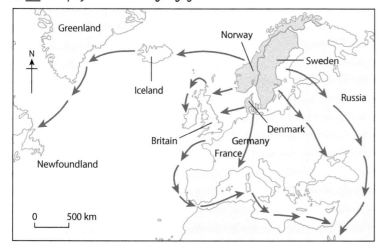

Work

1 Write a sentence or two to explain the following words: immigrant; empire.

2 Put the following groups of invaders and settlers into the correct chronological order: Romans; Anglo-Saxons; Celts; Vikings.

3 a Who were the Anglo-Saxons?
   b Why did Vikings begin to invade Britain in the eighth century?

What was 'Great' about King Alfred of Wessex?

Around the year 850, just like the Angle and Saxon tribes before them, the Vikings decided to settle in Britain. They landed along the eastern coast and built large, well-protected camps. Soon they started to venture out and capture British towns and villages. The city of York, for example, was captured in November 866 by an army of Danish Vikings. The Vikings slowly pushed their way across the country, and by 870, had conquered the Anglo-Saxon kingdoms of Northumbria, East Anglia and much of Mercia. What was their impact on the areas under Viking control? To what extent did the Anglo-Saxons, especially Alfred of Wessex, resist the Vikings?

Objectives

▶ **Describe** who Alfred the Great was, and his successes as King of Wessex.

▶ **Explain** how the Danelaw was created.

▶ **Assess** the impact of Viking rule on Britain.

Why did the Vikings choose to settle in Britain?

Although the Vikings and Anglo-Saxons were now fighting each other, they had much in common. Both groups were farming people who had a history of conquering new land to improve their lives, for example. The Vikings realised that Britain offered more opportunities than their homelands: Norway was very hilly and it was a struggle to grow crops there, and Denmark's sandy soil limited the number of animals that could be reared. Scandinavia was also becoming overcrowded, so many left looking for a new life abroad. Recruiting young men into the Viking armies was relatively easy, since only eldest sons inherited farmland, so younger brothers needed to join the army and make their own wealth by moving to other lands.

What happened to Wessex?

After conquering Northumbria, East Anglia and most of Mercia, the Vikings now turned their attention to Wessex. In 871, Alfred, the 22-year-old son of Aethelred of Wessex, had become king after his father's death. He would go on to be known as Alfred the Great. In 876, the Vikings began a series of ferocious attacks against Alfred's Wessex. After some early successes, King Alfred and his army were driven back and forced to hide on the Isle of Athelney in the Somerset marshes.

After several desperate months, Alfred managed to gather enough support and train an army to attack the Vikings once more. In May 878, King Alfred beat the Vikings at the Battle of Edington in Wiltshire, and the two sides sat down to agree peace terms. Alfred insisted that the Viking leader, Guthrum, had to become a Christian, like Alfred himself, and had to agree never to attack Wessex again. Alfred accepted that the Vikings were here to stay, and the two leaders settled on a boundary between their territories. The Vikings were to live in the north and east of the country (which was called the **Danelaw**).

▼ **A** *The division of Britain at the end of the ninth century. The map shows the Danelaw, where the Vikings conquered and settled, and Alfred's kingdom of Wessex.*

Danelaw

Wessex

The Danelaw

The part of England under Viking control changed considerably at this time. The Vikings brought their own distinct laws, place names, customs, measurements, skilled crafts and farming techniques to the Danelaw. Many of these Viking influences still survive today. For example, some days of our week have Viking names: Thursday is named after Thor, the Norse god of thunder;

King Alfred (reigned 871–99)

- Became the sixth King of Wessex in 871.

- Cultured and academic by ninth century standards, he encouraged learning and said that all young noble men should learn to read English. He translated many books from Latin into English.

- Re-wrote many laws. He took the most just laws from other kingdoms and used them for his.

- To ensure there would be no further Viking attacks in his lifetime, Alfred built burhs (fortresses or castles) across the country from the 880s to strengthen England's defences. The soldiers in these burhs could not only defend Alfred's land in Wessex, they could launch attacks if required. He also fortified existing Roman-era towns such as Oxford. As a result, Alfred had a grid of defensive sites across his territory that made his land more secure. Most importantly, his new defences showed confidence: they gave a sign to the Vikings that invasions were no longer as easy as before.

- Other kingdoms in England acknowledged Alfred to be the 'overlord', or the dominant ruler over them. Under his rule, the Anglo-Saxons began to call themselves Angelcynn – the English.

▼ **B** *Alfred is remembered as an Anglo-Saxon king who was a 'Great' general in war, a wise and kindly ruler in peace, and a clever scholar. This statue of him was put up in Winchester, his capital, 1000 years after his death.*

Friday after Freya, the goddess of love. Viking settlements can easily be detected through the use of the suffix 'by' (meaning 'homestead' or 'village'), for example Grimsby ('Grim's homestead'), or 'thorpe' (meaning 'new village'), or 'thwaite' (meaning 'meadow' or 'piece of land'). Some British surnames have Viking origins too (such as Adamson, Holt and Thorn), as do many words, such as egg, bread, sister, happy, ill and muck.

After Alfred

During Alfred's reign, there were still Viking raids on Anglo-Saxon territory. For the most part, however, the Vikings in the Danelaw settled down as farmers and lived fairly peacefully side-by-side with the Anglo-Saxons. People travelled and traded between Wessex and the Danelaw, and there was intermarriage between Vikings and Anglo-Saxons.

After Alfred's death, his descendants managed to re-capture parts of the Danelaw and win control over it. Alfred's grandson (Athelstan) conquered Northumbria in 927, and some historians argue that Athelstan could be called the first real 'King of England'. However, the Viking presence and influence still remained: York had Viking rulers until 954, for example. But by the time Alfred's great-grandson (Edgar the Peaceful) became king in 959, the country was as settled as it had been for generations.

Work

1 Why did the Vikings choose to settle in Britain?

2 a Who was Alfred?
   b How did Alfred gain the upper hand over the Vikings?
   c Why do you think Alfred is known by many as 'Alfred the Great'?

3 What was the Danelaw?

4 Describe the impact of the Vikings on Britain.

Extension

Find out more about what happened at the Battle of Eddington in 878 – who were the leaders, the tactics, and what happened in the battle?

Practice Question

Explain the significance of Alfred the Great for the development of English identity.   **8 marks**

Study Tip

Remember to refer to several aspects of Alfred's achievements and the impact they had for a long time after he had died.

Cnut, Emma and the North Sea Empire

In the ninth century, Alfred the Great had prevented the Vikings taking over all of England. After winning the Battle of Edington in 878, he made a peace treaty that restricted the Vikings to living only in the north and east of the country, an area known as the Danelaw. In the tenth century the English re-conquered much of the land held by the Vikings. Under King Edgar the Peaceful, the country became both calm and stable; but when he died in 975, things began to unravel. Within 50 years, England had a Viking king once more, and the country became part of the Danish Empire.

Objectives

▶ **Examine** the new Viking raiders of the late tenth century.

▶ **Explore** who King Cnut was and assess the way he controlled England.

▶ **Consider** the importance of Britain to Cnut's North Sea Empire, including the role of Emma of Normandy.

Edward then Aethelred

When King Edgar the Peaceful died, he left two sons by different mothers: Edward (aged 12) and Aethelred (aged 9). As the oldest son, Edward became King of England, but his reign only lasted three years. In 978, he was murdered by supporters of his younger brother Aethelred, who then took over as king.

Aethelred's reign was a difficult one. He was only a young boy when he became king, and was not a good judge of character. The advisers that helped him were often corrupt and looked to make as much money and acquire as much land as they could from the king. Many people were also outraged by the murder of his elder brother, Edward. There is little evidence that the young Aethelred had anything at all to do with his brother's death, but one story claims that his mother, Aelthfryth, stabbed Edward (her stepson) so that her own son could become king!

The Vikings return

During Aethelred's reign, new groups of Vikings searching for fame and fortune began to invade England. In 991, a huge Viking army, led by the Dane Sven Forkbeard and the Norwegian Olaf Tryggvason, arrived at Folkestone in a fleet of over 90 ships. Their army defeated the English at the Battle of Maldon in August. Aethelred paid the Vikings to

▼ **INTERPRETATION A** *A drawing, published in 1865, showing the victorious Vikings, after the Battle of Maldon, being paid Danegeld*

leave. The taxes raised to pay for this became known as **Danegeld** (money for the Danish). Not all of the Vikings left; some remained as mercenaries to protect the English and others continued to terrorise the English on the south coast for the next three years. After 997, fresh raiding parties of Vikings attacked parts of southern England. They demanded (and received) Danegeld.

Aethelred and Emma of Normandy

The Danegeld that Aethelred was paying the Vikings to stay away from England was costing a fortune. After the Battle of Maldon, the king had given the Vikings around 3300 kilogrammes of silver (about £1.8 million in today's money), and the English hated the taxes that were needed to pay it. As a result, Aethelred looked for another way to keep the Vikings away.

The Vikings had been sheltering in Normandy, France, after raiding England. The Normans were descendants of Vikings who had settled in France around 100 years before. So, Aethelred made a deal with the Duke of Normandy that said that they agreed to support each other against their enemies. Aethelred hoped that this would reduce the number of raids because the Vikings would not be able to use Normandy as a base. Aethelred sealed the agreement by marrying the Duke's sister, Emma. However, in November 1002 Aethelred used the popular fear and hatred of the Vikings to carry out a mass killing of all Viking men, women and children that he could find south of the Danelaw. This became known as the St Brice's Day Massacre and caused the anger of King Sven Forkbeard, whose sister Gunhilda was murdered.

Forkbeard attacks

The King of Denmark, Sven Forkbeard, invaded England with a powerful Viking army. He wanted revenge – and some of the great wealth of England for himself. If he achieved this it would strengthen his position against rival Viking leaders. In 1000 at the Battle of Svold, Sven killed Olaf Tryggvason, his former raiding partner who had become King of Norway. Sven also wanted to teach Thorkell the Tall a lesson. Thorkell was a Viking warrior who switched sides to work for Aethelred in 1012. In 1013, Sven summoned a large army and swiftly conquered England.

Cnut, Emma and the North Sea Empire

Aethelred and Cnut

With Aethelred out of the country and Forkbeard on the throne, it looked as if the fighting between Anglo-Saxons and Vikings was over for a while. But the peace didn't last. Just over a year after becoming king, Forkbeard died. His young son, Cnut (pronounced Canute), became England's new Viking king, but Anglo-Saxon nobles wanted the Anglo-Saxon Aethelred to return to power. Aethelred came back over to England in 1014 and forced Cnut back to Denmark. Aethelred was now back on the throne.

Edmund and Cnut

Aethelred's return did not last long. Cnut's supporters in England rebelled against Aethelred, and the next few years involved much bloodshed and fighting. At one point, even Aethelred's own son rebelled against him. In April 1016, Aethelred died and his son, Edmund, became king. He was successful in fighting off Vikings, and earned himself the nickname 'Edmund Ironside'. However, in October 1016, Cnut finally got the better of King Edmund and beat him at the Battle of Assandun in Essex. The two men agreed that Edmund would run Wessex, while Cnut would run the rest of the country; and when one of them died, the other would inherit their land. About a month later, Edmund died. Historians believe he was either murdered or died from wounds received at the Battle of Assandun. Now Cnut became king of all England.

How did Britain change under Cnut's rule?

Britain was important to Cnut as it was his richest kingdom: he viewed Britain as his main domain, rather than as a Danish colony. To begin with, King Cnut was tough with those Anglo-Saxons he thought might rebel against him. Early in his reign, he ordered the execution of a number of powerful Anglo-Saxons. Britain was a rich area with a flourishing trade system compared to Scandinavia, and Cnut wanted to have reliable and strong

▼ **B** *Cnut's North Sea Empire*

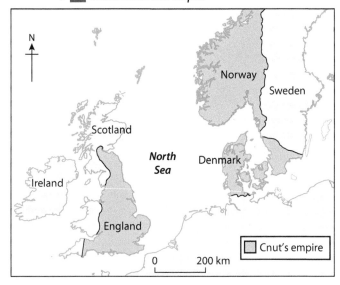

N

Norway

Sweden

Scotland

North Sea

Denmark

Ireland

England

☐ Cnut's empire

0   200 km

Key Biography

Cnut the Great (reigned as King of England 1016–35)

- Brought in an era of peace that lasted nearly 20 years.
- Was seen as a fair, just and devout ruler, and was popular overall.
- Made expensive payments to fund the part of the Viking army that stayed in England.
- Used money to pay for trusted Danish nobles to move to England to help him maintain order.
- Married Aethelred's widow, Emma of Normandy.
- Died in 1035, and was buried in Winchester.

> [In the 1040s], Canute was, with the single exception of the Emperor, the most imposing ruler in Latin Christendom... He was lord of four important realms and the overlord of other kingdoms. Though technically Canute was counted among the kings, his position among his fellow-monarchs was truly imperial. Apparently he held in his hands the destinies of two great regions: the British Isles and the Scandinavian peninsulas. His fleet all but controlled two important seas, the North and the Baltic. He had built an Empire.

leaders to help him control Britain. Strong control meant he could transfer the riches back to Denmark to support the Danes. Loyal Danish nobles were given British lands, but some trustworthy English nobles were also left to rule their own areas. Cnut wanted good local leadership – no matter which side of the North Sea they were from.

Despite a brutal takeover of the throne and start to his reign, Cnut's reign was one of peace and freedom from Viking raids. He even sent most of his great battle fleets home. He also worked hard to win over the people of his new kingdom. He was a religious man who established a good relationship with Church leaders, and he brought back many of the popular and fair laws of Edgar the Peaceful. Soon, he inherited the kingdoms of Denmark and Norway from his elder brother, and ruled parts of Sweden too. All of this is known by historians today as Cnut's North Sea Empire.

Cnut and Emma of Normandy

To bring even greater stability to England, and an improved relationship with the Normans in France, Cnut married Emma of Normandy, widow of Aethelred. They had a son, Harthacnut.

During Cnut's 20-year reign, England was at peace. But his two sons who followed him as king – firstly Harold (Cnut's son by his first wife) and then Harthacnut (his son with Emma) – were hated. Their reigns didn't last long. In 1042, Harthacnut died and the throne passed to his surviving half-brother, Prince Edward. Edward was the son of Emma and Aethlered, and had originally left with his mother and father when Forkbeard invaded many years before. He had been living in Normandy for much of his life. King Edward was quickly accepted by ordinary people, but the Anglo-Saxon nobles found that he seemed to prefer his Norman friends to them. He was also a deeply religious man and soon earned himself the nickname 'the Confessor': a name given to a person who lives a very holy life.

Fact

Emma of Normandy proved to be a strong leader who was respected and listened to when Cnut travelled in his empire. She also improved relations with the Church and helped to bring peace to England. She was renowned for being good with money – protecting not only Cnut's but her own interests.

▼ **SOURCE D** *An image from an eleventh century book showing Emma of Normandy receiving a book about her life. She is watched by her two sons.*

Work

1 Describe King Cnut's time as King of England.

2 Who was Edward the Confessor and why did he become King of England?

3 In what ways are the marriages and children of Emma of Normandy an important part of the history of this period?

4 a What was meant by the term 'North Sea Empire'?

   b Explain why Viking kings such as Cnut wanted to take over Britain. Why was Britain important?

   c How did Britain change under Cnut?

A Norman Kingdom

When Edward became King of England in 1042, he had been living in Normandy, France for many years. He spoke French better than he spoke English and behaved like a Norman. One of his closest friends was a Norman too. His name was William, the Duke (ruler) of Normandy, and King Edward spent lots of time in Normandy with him. But Edward had not married a Norman as people expected, and instead married the sister of a powerful Anglo-Saxon called Harold Godwinson. They had no children, and when Edward died in early 1066, the throne of England was up for grabs. With its wealth and land, England was worth fighting for. Who claimed the throne and became England's next king? And what did this mean for the country as a whole?

Objectives

▶ **Recall** what happened after King Edward's death.

▶ **Examine** the way in which England became part of a Norman Empire.

▶ **Explore** the relationship between England and France from 1066 to 1216.

The race for the crown

King Edward died on 6 January 1066. The three main contenders for the English throne were:

- William, Duke of Normandy: As a close friend of Edward, he claimed that he been promised the throne. He also claimed that Harold Godwinson had agreed to support his claim after being rescued from a shipwreck off the coast of Normandy.
- Harald Hardrada: The Viking ruler of Norway; he also said he was King of Denmark. As Vikings had conquered and controlled England for many years, he claimed he should be England's new king.
- Harold Godwinson: By now, Harold was the most powerful man in England; and he was English, unlike the other two. He was a good soldier and the council of the country's most important, powerful nobles (known as the **Witan**) wanted him as king.

The day after Edward's death, the Witan elected Harold as king. He was crowned immediately; but when the other two rivals found out, they planned their invasions. Hardrada the Viking was the first to invade, but was defeated by King Harold at the Battle of Stamford Bridge, near York, in September 1066. A few days later, King Harold heard the news that William of Normandy had landed on the south coast of England. Harold rushed south from Yorkshire to fight him, but was defeated at the Battle of Hastings on 14 October 1066. Over the next few weeks, William faced fierce resistance from the English as they moved from Hastings towards London, but William soon crushed any resistance on his way there, and was crowned as the first Norman King of England on Christmas Day, 1066.

▼ **INTERPRETATION A** *A fourteenth-century illustration of William killing Harold at the Battle of Hastings*

William completes the conquest

Even though he had been crowned King of England, William couldn't relax. The early years of his reign saw major rebellions up and down the country. These were put down fiercely. The king rewarded his most loyal

Norman followers by giving them important jobs in the Church, and by seizing land from the English and giving it to Normans. Soon, England was divided up between Norman **barons** and lords, each with his own knights and soldiers to keep the peace. This meant that William would have people loyal to him to control the country during the times when he returned to Normandy. These barons and knights built castles to keep them safe from any English rebels who might want to attack them. Soon England had over 500 Norman castles.

▼ **SOURCE B** *A Norman writer, recalling what became known as the 'Harrying (destruction) of the North' in 1070*

> Never had William shown so great a cruelty. He assembled crops, herds and flocks, food and utensils of every kind and burned them all. Then all sources of life north of the Humber were destroyed. There followed a famine so serious that more than 100,000 of all ages and both sexes perished.

A Norman Kingdom

William was a French prince who had acquired the English kingdom, but he spent more than half his time in France, where he felt at home. It was very important for William to be seen in France because powerful French rivals might take advantage of any absences to seize control of Normandy. But William spared no time in stamping his mark on England too. The Normans became a brand-new ruling class in England. They spoke French and introduced French customs. They built hundreds of new churches, cathedrals and monasteries, and French replaced English as the main language used by the people in power. Hundreds of French words such as soldier, parliament, royal, city, minister and army were soon absorbed into the English language. The English were once again ruled by a foreign power: the land they once owned was taken from them and the taxes they paid went to the Normans. The Anglo-Saxon English became second-class citizens.

▼ **C** *The Norman Kingdom; the Normans didn't try to conquer Scotland, but had a strong influence over it*

Fact

Like the Vikings, the Normans focused their efforts on England, but they did have an impact on people from Scotland and Wales. King Malcolm of Scotland raided England in 1070. William's response was violent. He invaded Scotland in 1072 and Malcolm recognised William's power and made peace. William did not attempt to conquer all of Wales, but instructed several Norman barons to seize land there.

Work

1   Explain why you think William, Hardrada and Harold each thought they had a right to be King of England.
2   After becoming king, what did William do with England?
3   How did England change under Norman rule? Make sure you mention: language, castles, the English people.

Practice Question

How useful is **Source B** to a historian studying the Norman attitude to England?   **8 marks**

Study Tip

The provenance says the author is a Norman writer from the time. Does knowing who the author is affect what historians think about the source?

2.2 Henry II and the 'Angevin' Empire

In 1087, William the Conqueror died and his Norman Kingdom was divided up between his two eldest sons. Robert (the eldest) became Duke of Normandy, and William's middle son (William) became William II of England. The youngest son, Henry, got nothing. But in 1100, William II died and Henry took over as King of England. He then went on to defeat his older brother too, and became Duke of Normandy in 1106. So once again the Norman Kingdom was united under one man: Henry I of England and Duke of Normandy.

Objectives

▶ **Explain** who the 'Angevins' were.

▶ **Describe** the territory Henry II controlled in Britain and France.

▶ **Examine** how Henry's territory increased in size during his reign, including the invasion of Ireland.

King Henry ruled peacefully for 20 years. He wanted his daughter, Matilda, to rule England after him when he died. He married her to a powerful French lord, Geoffrey of Anjou. But when Henry died, a powerful noble named Stephen seized the throne. Stephen was Henry's nephew and a grandson of William the Conqueror, so many people thought he had a right to the throne. Matilda decided to fight back, however, and for the next 19 years there was a series of battles between the two. Finally, in 1153, an agreement was reached that Matilda's son, Henry, would become England's next king, after Stephen's death. So when Stephen died in October 1154, Matilda's son became King Henry II of England.

Henry II: not just England's king

Henry II was not just King of England: he inherited Normandy from his mother, Matilda, as well as other land in France from his father, Geoffrey of Anjou. As a result, Henry II was King of England, Duke of Normandy, Count of Anjou and Count of Maine. In 1152, he married a French duchess, Eleanor of Aquitaine, which meant that he also gained the largest region in his domain: the territories of Aquitaine stretched all the way to Spain. He even bought some areas of France, bullied his way into controlling others, and married his son off to a French duchess so he could acquire Brittany – another powerful, large area of northern France. In fact, Henry II was arguably one of the most powerful rulers in Europe, with land stretching from the Scottish borders to the south of France. He would soon also count Ireland in his empire too.

Invasion of Ireland

Some of the early Norman kings (such as William the Conqueror and Henry I) showed little interest in conquering Ireland. The Irish Sea was rough and difficult to cross, and Ireland wasn't a particularly rich country, so the English felt they wouldn't gain much from taking it over. Ireland was governed by nobles who styled themselves as 'kings'.

But in 1166, 'King' Dermot of Leinster, the leader of Leinster, an area in Ireland, asked Henry II for help. He was fighting

▼ **INTERPRETATION A** *King Henry II, shown in a portrait painted in 1620*

another Irish 'king' and wanted Henry's assistance. An army of English knights and barons led by the Earl of Pembroke – nicknamed 'Strongbow' – crossed over to Ireland and helped the Irish leader. However, the knights and barons took the opportunity to seize land in Ireland for themselves when Dermot died in 1171 and, within a few years, controlled more land than the Irish. Henry II himself visited Ireland in 1171 and was recognised as the 'overlord' by all the English settlers and the Irish leaders. In fact, this 'deal' became the basis of English sovereignty over the Irish for hundreds of years, up to the 1940s.

Henry's work in Ireland continued as he strengthened existing fortifications there and built new castles, as well as getting investors to develop Dublin as a centre of trade and commerce.

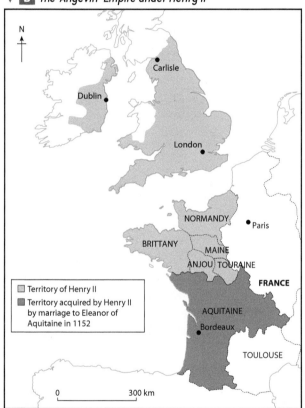

▼ **B** *The 'Angevin' Empire under Henry II*

Key:
- ☐ Territory of Henry II
- ☐ Territory acquired by Henry II by marriage to Eleanor of Aquitaine in 1152

A well-travelled king

At this time, France was not a united country, as it is today. It was divided into areas, each ruled by powerful lords and dukes. France itself was one of these areas, ruled by a king, but other areas included Anjou, Aquitaine, Normandy and Brittany. Henry II of England ruled over half of these areas, but not France, which was a large, powerful area ruled by King Louis VII. However, Henry II ruled more French land than Louis. With so much land to defend, Henry II spent much of his reign crossing between England and France. It has been estimated that Henry crossed the English Channel up to 30 times in his 35-year reign, prompting Louis VII to remark that Henry 'must fly rather than travel by horse or ship'. There was conflict between Henry II and Louis VII during their reigns too. There was a war in Normandy in 1167, for example, and Louis joined in when Henry's own sons rebelled against him in 1173.

Work

1 Describe the circumstances in which Henry II became King of England.

2 Why is Henry II described as the 'first "Angevin" King of England'?

3 Explain why the first 'Angevin' King of England ruled over more territory than his Norman predecessors.

4 Look at map **B**.
   a Use the scale to work out how far it is from Carlisle (in the north of England) to Bordeaux (in the south of the 'Angevin' Empire).
   b How long would it take to travel there by horse, at 50 kilometres a day?
   c Why might this be a problem for Henry II?

5 Describe how Henry II gradually became 'overlord' of Ireland by 1171.

Fact

The 'Angevins' and the Plantagenets

Henry II (and his brothers who ruled after him) are often referred to as the 'Angevins'. This is because their father Geoffrey came from Anjou in France. Later, the family became known as the Plantagenets because Geoffrey famously wore a yellow plant, *planta genista*, in his hat.

Practice Question

Explain the significance of Henry II's empire. **8 marks**

Study Tip

Refer to King Henry II's relationship with Ireland then and Anglo-Irish relations today.

Why did the 'Angevin' Empire collapse under King John?

When Henry II died in 1189, he was replaced as king by his son, Richard I. Richard spent long periods of his reign in his French lands, or on **crusades** to the Holy Land. As a result, the 'Angevin' Empire became hard to govern. Richard had to return to England to stop rebellions, but he couldn't prevent the French King Philip II from taking large areas of his land in France, including part of Normandy. Richard I died in 1199. His younger brother, John, became the new king, but things got gradually worse. What happened to the 'Angevin' Empire under King John?

Objectives

▶ **Describe** the losses of territories under King John.

▶ **Explain** the causes of John's 'Angevin' Empire becoming smaller.

▶ **Analyse** the impact of losses under King John.

King John's opponents

King John had an opponent waiting to take control of some of his French lands. Powerful lords in Brittany and Anjou wanted John's young nephew, Arthur, as king, and John was drawn into a series of battles against him to defend his land. Arthur also had the support of John's rival, the French King Philip II. But in 1203, Arthur died in mysterious circumstances: many suspected that John stabbed him and threw his body in the River Seine.

King Philip II of France continued his campaign against John, and invaded Anjou and Normandy. In 1204, John's army was defeated in Brittany and began to retreat. Over the next few years, John lost Normandy, Anjou, Maine and other key areas. His military reputation reached such a low point that he was given a new nickname: 'John Softsword'. Soon, John had hardly any land left in France.

▼ **SOURCE A** *An illustration from c1200 showing King John on a stag hunt*

Timeline

1150	1151	1152	1154	1166–68	1171–72	1189
Henry inherits Normandy from his mother, Matilda, four years before he becomes King Henry II of England	Henry succeeds his father, Geoffrey, as Count of Anjou, Maine, and Touraine in France	Henry marries Eleanor of Aquitaine, and through this marriage he acquires Aquitaine, which includes Gascony, Poitou and Auvergne	Henry becomes King Henry II of England	Henry II invades Brittany	Henry II invades Ireland	Henry II dies and his son becomes Richard I. He goes on a crusade leaving England to be ruled by two justicians (special judges or ministers)

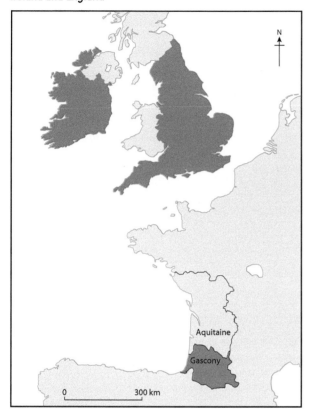

▼ **B** *By 1214, the 'Angevin' Empire had been reduced to only Gascony (the southern half of the Duchy of Aquitaine), Ireland and England*

Aquitaine

Gascony

0   300 km

More losses of territories under King John

After the defeats in France, John went back to England. He attempted to raise an army to invade France and take back the land. But this meant raising taxes to pay for it, which made him very unpopular. After another defeat in France in 1214, the English barons decided to take action against their king. Taxes were higher than ever and French lands such as Normandy, Brittany, Anjou and Maine were no longer under John's control. By now, his land

Key Words

crusade   Magna Carta

in France consisted of just one area – Gascony. So the barons rebelled by putting together their own army and marching towards London, to take over. They gave John a choice: change the way he was running the country, or fight the army that was heading towards London. King John gave in and asked the barons what they wanted. John eventually agreed to their demands, set out in a document called **Magna Carta** (Great Charter). He promised, among other things, to respect the rights of the Church and the barons, to stop unfair taxes, and to ensure that trials would be held quickly and fairly.

Work

1 a In what ways did the 'Angevin' Empire decline during the reign of Richard I?
   b Can you suggest reasons for the decline?
2 a Who was 'John Softsword'?
   b Why do you think he was given this nickname?
3 Create a presentation, poster or write an extended answer that describes the rise and fall of the 'Angevin' Empire. Make sure you use dates, names of territories and kings in your description. You might want to use maps to give an extra visual dimension to your work.

Extension

How did King John's problems with his 'Angevin' Empire help lead to Magna Carta?

1193–94	1199	1202–05	1204–14	1216
John schemes with King Philip II of France to undermine King Richard: Philip of France invades Normandy and Anjou	Richard I is killed; his brother becomes King John. John and Arthur of Brittany in conflict over land in France; Arthur is murdered	Philip II conquers Normandy, Anjou, Maine and Brittany	King John tries to regain control of Normandy	John dies, and with the loss of Anjou and many other important French lands, this marks the end of the 'Angevin' Empire. King John was an inadequate military leader who did not inspire loyalty. His involvement in the murder of Arthur of Brittany shocked and alienated many of his important subjects. Henry II had been rich, but due to the high cost of Richard I's wars, England was financially exhausted by 1199. King John lost an empire through bad decisions and because he ran out of money at a crucial time

3.1 The Hundred Years War

William the Conqueror was both King of England and Duke of Normandy. He spent most of his time up to 1072 in England, and then spent the majority of his time in Normandy. In fact, the early Norman kings of England (who were often based in Normandy) just regarded England as part of an empire they ruled. These kings also brought much of Wales and Scotland under their control and influence. Some kings of England, such as Henry II, were successful in gaining more land from the French. However, most of this land was eventually won back by the French during the reign of King John (1199–1216). By the time Edward III became King of England in 1327, only Gascony and a small part of northern France remained under the King of England's control.

Objectives

▶ **Outline** the Anglo-French relationship before the Hundred Years War began.

▶ **Examine** why the Hundred Years War started.

▶ **Evaluate** which cause of the war was the most important.

Causes of war

▼ **SOURCE A** *King Edward at his coronation in 1327, from an early fourteenth century illuminated manuscript*

In 1337, King Edward III of England claimed the French throne and declared war on France. He was 24 years old and was determined to be a stronger ruler than his father, Edward II. The young king saw a war with France as a way of achieving glory on the battlefield; but there were other reasons why war broke out:

- England still controlled the Gascony area of France, where a lot of wine was made. When the wine was taken to England it was taxed, and King Edward made lots of money from this. However, the French threatened to take over this wine producing area.

- England sold lots of wool abroad. Areas near France (for example, Flanders) turned this wool into cloth. Both the English and the people in places like Flanders made lots of money doing this. But the French threatened to take over these areas. If the wool trade was stopped, it would make England poorer, and people wouldn't be able to afford to pay King Edward so much tax.

- Edward was closely linked to France. His grandfather had been King of France and his mother was the daughter of a French king. He thought he had a better claim to the throne of France than the French king at the time, Philip VI.

- Edward was in conflict with Scotland at this time. The French promised to help the Scots, which made Edward furious!

The Hundred Years War

In 1337, England and France started fighting to gain control of the French throne. Known as the Hundred Years War, the war lasted, off and on, until 1453 (a total of 116 years) and covered the reigns of five English kings. There were battles at sea, but most of the fighting was done on French land. None of the fighting happened in England.

The Hundred Years War can be divided into three distinct phases, separated by truces. The first stage of the war lasted from 1337 until 1360 and it went particularly well for the English. Edward III won important battles at Crécy (1346) and Poitiers (1356) and captured the French port of Calais, the nearest large port to England. Calais remained in English hands for the next 200 years. Edward also captured the French king and held him to ransom. After this, the fighting died down. Edward gave up his demands to the French throne in return for the right to control Gascony, Calais and other minor French territories.

The second stage of the war began in 1370, when the French won back some of the land they had lost. Then the final phase of war began in 1413 when Henry V became England's king. His victory at the Battle of Agincourt in 1415 led to his conquest of much of northern France, including Normandy. But Henry V died in 1422 and was succeeded by his nine-month-old son. Soon, the gains made under Henry V were swept away. Joan of Arc, a 17-year-old French peasant girl, believed she had been chosen by God to lead the French to victory. She led the army that defeated the English at the Siege of Orléans in 1429. Inspired by this pious and courageous girl, the French beat the English forces time and time again. By the end of the war in 1453, the English had lost all their territory in France except for the tiny area around Calais. Joan was burned at the stake by the English in 1431.

Work

1 a How many years did the Hundred Years War last?
  b Why do you think it was called the Hundred Years War?

2 Look at the two maps in **B**. In your own words, explain how the French territory under England's control changed between 1360 and 1453.

3 In your opinion, who won the Hundred Years War? Give reasons for your answer.

Fact

Every English king between 1199 and 1461 married a French princess or noblewoman, but marriage didn't always bring peace between the two countries.

◀ ▼ **B** *Maps showing the height of English territorial gains during the Hundred Years War (in 1360), and how little territory the English had at the end of the war (in 1453)*

Practice Question

Were economic factors the main cause of the Hundred Years War?

16 marks
SPaG: 4 marks

Study Tip

Write about personal reasons as well as economic ones in your answer.

Extension

Research the reign of Edward II and produce a fact file of his achievements. Why was Edward III determined to be more successful?

The impact of the Hundred Years War

3.2A

The Hundred Years War was not one long war, but a series of battles that lasted from 1337 to 1453. There were many years of little or no fighting, when both sides made peace deals, and times when there were major, aggressive campaigns by one side or another. This war gave both France and England some of their best-known heroes and greatest victories. One of the most notable battles in the later phase of the war occurred on 25 October 1415 near Agincourt, France. It was fought between the heavily outnumbered army of King Henry V of England and that of King Charles VI of France. Why was the Battle of Agincourt so important? And what was the impact of the battle, and of the Hundred Years War, on the birth of English identity?

Objectives

▶ **Recall** the importance of the Battle of Agincourt.

▶ **Analyse** the impact of the Hundred Years War for both England and France.

▶ **Assess** how the war contributed to the birth of English identity.

The Battle of Agincourt

Twenty-five-year-old Henry V became King of England in 1413. Two years later, he sailed for France, which was to be the focus of his attention for the rest of his reign. Henry was determined to regain the territories in France that former kings of England had lost. Soon after arriving in France, he captured Harfleur, a port in Normandy. But Henry lost half his men to disease and battle injuries, so decided to march his army north to Calais, where he would meet a fleet of English ships and return to England. But the French had no intention of letting Henry get away: at Agincourt, a vast French army of 30,000 men stood in his path.

▼ **INTERPRETATION A** *An interpretation of King Henry V (in the crown) at the Battle of Agincourt, from a book about English history published in England in 1864*

Approximately 11,000 exhausted English archers, knights and foot soldiers were there, and they were outnumbered three to one.

The battle took place in a field that lay between two woods. It had rained heavily before the battle: this, combined with the fact that the field had recently been ploughed, would have a major impact on the outcome of the battle. Fighting began around 11:00am on 25 October 1415. **Diagrams B** and **C** show two stages in the battle.

Fact

The archers that fought for Henry used large bows called longbows. They could fire around 12 arrows a minute and could kill a man nearly 200 metres away. The French tended to use crossbows, which were very powerful and accurate, but took longer to load. The archers proved decisive at Agincourt, as they had done at the Battle of Crécy in 1346. The humble, common archer was now more than a match for the powerful knight on horseback.

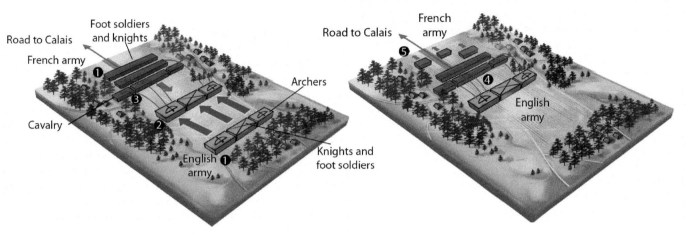

1 English and French positions at start of the Battle of Agincourt.

2 Henry immediately moved his troops forward and ordered his archers to open fire.

3 The French tried to charge at the English, but a combination of thick mud, heavy armour and wooden spikes that the English had set up in front of themselves slowed them down.

4 The French continued to charge, but they were bogged down in the mud and unable to advance. The English archers continued their attack from above and slaughtered the French.

5 The battle was a disaster for the French; the survivors fled.

Consequences of the battle

Estimates suggest that the French lost between 7000 and 10,000 men at Agincourt, while the English lost only a few hundred. After the victory, Henry V went on to conquer Normandy and tighten his grip on France. Many powerful French knights and nobles were killed at Agincourt and, before long, the daughter of the French king had become Henry's wife, as part of the Treaty of Troyes, 1420. The treaty, which was a direct result of English military success, made Henry V heir to the French throne; but he never lived to be king of a united England and France. In 1422, aged just 35, Henry died suddenly of dysentery. Soon after, French fortunes began to turn. Inspired by Joan of Arc, who claimed that voices of the saints had called on her to free France from the English, the French gradually began to drive the English out. The English caught Joan of Arc, accused her of witchcraft and burned her to death, but over the next few decades, the French regained most of the territories occupied by the English.

Work

1 Why was there a battle at Agincourt?

2 Look at **Interpretation A**.
   a What impression do you get of Henry V from this picture?
   b Consider the provenance (caption). Can you suggest reasons why Henry is portrayed like this?

3 You have been asked to design a page on the battle for a children's history book, aimed at children under 11. Plan out the page on A4 paper and, in under 200 words, write a simple description suitable for children of this age.

Extension

Agincourt is not the only famous battle to take place during the Hundred Years War. Research another famous battle that took place (such as the Battle of Crécy or the Battle of Poitiers), and consider its significance.

The impact of the Hundred Years War

The legacy of the Hundred Years War

Historians often debate about whether or not an event, individual or issue is significant. When historians see something as significant, it means more than just that it is important. The following criteria are commonly used when assessing historical significance:

- Impact at the time: Was the event, person, development or issue important at the time? How deeply were people's lives affected? How many lives were affected?
- Impact in the long term: For how long have people's lives been affected? Is the event, person, development or issue still relevant in today's world?

So, when exploring the impact of the Hundred Years War, it is important to think about these questions so you can judge whether the war was a significant event, and how significant it is!

Fact

Historians have found it very difficult to put a number on the amount of soldiers and civilians who died during the conflict as a result of battle disease, and famine. Estimates range from 180,000 to over three million.

▼ **SOURCE D** *A painting of the Battle of Poitiers in the Hundred Years War, from* Froissart's Chronicles, *written in the fourteenth century*

Impact on France and England at the time

Some areas of France (for example, Normandy) were devastated during the fighting. Armies on both sides seized crops and animals, and stole whatever riches they could find. If an army was retreating, they might burn all the buildings they left behind so their advancing enemy couldn't use them. Lots of ordinary men fought (and died) on both sides too, although there were fewer battle casualties on the English side. Many English deaths were from dysentery, rather than destruction on the battlefield.

The cost of war

The high cost of weapons, food, armour and horses meant that wars were very expensive. As a result, both the French and English had to pay higher taxes, more frequently, to pay for the war. By the end of the war, England had lost wealthy French regions like Normandy and Aquitaine, so could no longer make money from these areas. However, some Englishmen got very rich from the stolen goods taken from France. Bodiam Castle in Sussex, for example, was built from the proceeds made from the war.

The military impact

The war changed the way battles were fought. Before the Hundred Years War, the knight on horseback, fighting as part of the cavalry, was the most effective, powerful and feared part of an army. However, it was the archers, firing thousands of arrows, that led to the great French defeats at Crécy, Poitiers and Agincourt. This spelled the end of the dominance of the knight on horseback. From then on, the power of missile fire, first from the longbow and later from the handgun, was the most effective battle technique. Soon, the ordinary foot soldiers were the key element to an army, rather than the cavalry. The war also saw the increased use of gunpowder, cannons and handguns. And as soon as gunpowder was used regularly, castles proved to be of little use in battles, so they began a long decline.

French unity

France had long been a collection of separate territories – Normandy, Aquitaine, Brittany and Gascony, for example. But a great number of the powerful, important French nobles who controlled these areas were killed during the war. As a result, the King of France emerged more powerful than ever. He was the one central leader of the country, and the French people rallied behind him.

The Hundred Years War led to a surge in nationalist feelings among the French: a love of their country and a love of their king! Also, the high cost of paying for the war led the French to set up a better system of taxing the whole country: this was so successful that they were able to pay for the first full-time army in Europe.

The birth of English identity

England and France had been connected since the days when William, Duke of Normandy defeated Harold to become the King of England. The Hundred Years War caused the two countries to forge their own identities. During the course of the war, England stopped using French as its official court language, because it was seen as the 'enemy language'.

After losing its territory in France, England became less involved in relations with the rest of Europe. England began to see itself as 'apart' from Europe, rather than a part of it. A much more unified country developed against the French, Scots and everyone else; and Crécy, Agincourt and other major battles gave the English a sense of pride and a unique identity. With a common language and homeland, a sense of what it meant to be 'English' quickly developed. Kings started to use the English language, and people started speaking of themselves as 'English' – not just from a region of England.

England's outlook and aims changed too: it was now a country looking to conquer lands outside Europe, a country that would soon look to develop an empire in newly found lands.

Work

1 In your own words, explain the impact of the Hundred Years War on the following:
   - England and France at the time
   - the way wars were fought in the future
   - the French monarchy
   - the English language.

2 a What do you think is meant by the term 'English identity'?
   b Why might the Hundred Years War be seen as a major factor in the birth of English identity?

3 In what ways was the Hundred Years War a 'significant' event? Use the criteria on this page to help you with your judgement.

Practice Question

Explain two ways in which the impact on Britain of the Hundred Years War and the Viking invasions of Britain were similar. **8 marks**

Study Tip

Consider the consequences of both events for different groups of people in Britain.

Why did Tudor and Stuart explorers look west?

The age of the Tudor and Stuart monarchs was one of momentous change. Under the Tudors, England and Wales were finally united and large parts of Ireland came under direct English control. The Tudors and the Scottish royal family, the Stuarts, came together through marriage too, and later the two countries united under one king. For many, Britain became a more prosperous place as farming and industry expanded. There was also a surge in overseas trade, as British explorers and even pirates found new sea routes across the Atlantic and Indian Oceans. These adventurers laid strong foundations for an overseas empire.

Objectives

▶ **Describe** the westward explorations of English sailors.

▶ **Explain** the consequences of this expansion.

The New World: overseas exploration

▼ **A** *Maps of the known world in Tudor and Stuart times, in 1480 and in 1600*

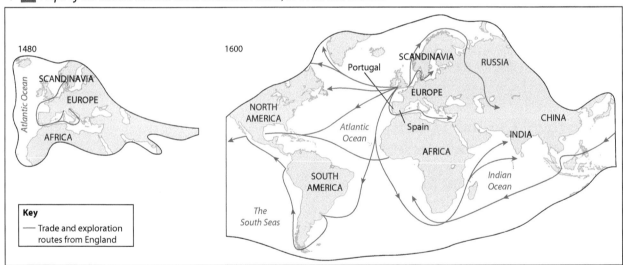

In the late 1400s, improvements in technology for ships and navigation meant longer journeys were possible, and more ships returned from these journeys. In 1492, Christopher Columbus (who was working for the Spanish) set sail across the Atlantic Ocean, hoping to find new routes to India and China by sea. Instead, by sailing west, he 'discovered' a group of islands in the Caribbean that Europeans didn't know existed – European colonisers later named them the 'West Indies'. In fact, he had found the continents we now know as the Americas. Soon more explorers from Spain, and then Portugal, set sail for the Americas to claim land for their monarchs.

Spain was the first major nation to **colonise** the Americas. The Spanish discovered gold in South America, which made them rich. In 1496, the Tudor King Henry VII joined this age of exploration when he gave the adventurer John Cabot the mission of finding new lands.

From the port of Bristol, Cabot sailed westwards across the Atlantic, and landed on the coast of North America in what is now Canada. But there were no great riches or obvious financial gains to be found in this newly discovered place – no silks and no gold – so Cabot returned home. However, Cabot's brief visit marked the start of the British Empire. Over time, British settlers would move out to live in what was named 'Newfoundland', and eventually settle all along the east coast of North America. Establishing a base now meant that other British adventurers, such as Sir John Hawkins

Sir John Hawkins (1532–95)

An artist's impression of the coat of arms of John Hawkins

- Was the second son of William Hawkins, who sailed in trading expeditions to West Africa in the 1530s.
- His first voyages were to the Spanish Canary Islands in the Atlantic. He became a respected English naval commander, merchant, **privateer** and pirate, and was responsible for building up the Elizabethan Royal Navy.
- Became Britain's first slave trader. In 1562, financed by a group of London merchants, he set sail on his first slave-trading voyage, capturing Africans to sell in the Americas. The voyage was so profitable that another group, including Queen Elizabeth I, provided the money for a second trip in 1564.
- Was the cousin of another well-known explorer, Sir Francis Drake, who joined him in his slave-trading activities.
- Included an image, on the crest of his coat of arms, of an enslaved African who is bound.
- Knighted by Queen Elizabeth I during the Spanish Armada in 1588.

colonise   privateer   plunder   piracy

and Sir Walter Raleigh, could explore and claim further territory. They could also **plunder** riches from Spanish ships and colonies.

It is important to note that there was a religious dimension to the competition between Spain and England at this time – Spain was Catholic and England was Protestant. This religious rivalry gave an added edge to the desire of each country's monarch to gain more land and increase their power base.

Piracy and plunder

As Britain failed to find any of its own gold, it used other methods: one of the ways in which countries obtained wealth and riches at this time was simply by taking it from another country's ships or territory. Any sailor with permission from the king or queen – known as a privateer – could attack foreign ships and steal from them. This permission was granted as long as the privateers shared anything they stole with the monarch. Any sailors who didn't have permission, and kept any treasure for themselves, were known as pirates. An estimated 10 to 15 per cent of all Spanish treasure ships were successfully captured by rival countries. Some successful British privateers also took part in **piracy** – keeping the plunder for themselves rather than sharing it with the monarch.

Extension

Research the life of a famous English privateer, such as Sir Francis Drake, Sir Walter Raleigh or Sir Henry Morgan.

Work

1   Describe the circumstances in which Columbus found the Americas.
2   What is the difference between a privateer and a pirate?
3   Why did Britain invest in privateering and piracy against the Spanish Empire in the Tudor and Stuart eras?
4   Why was Cabot's voyage important?

Why was piracy replaced by plantations?

Explorers like Drake, Hawkins and Morgan made lots of money for Britain as privateers, by stealing fortunes from Spanish and Portuguese ships. However, by the late 1500s, it became clear that there were other ways to make money out of the **New World** of the Americas. Britain set up colonies there, and by the 1600s, developed huge farms called **plantations**, where crops like sugar and cotton were grown. Where were the plantations set up, and who would do the hard work of farming the crops?

Objectives

▶ **Explain** why Britain moved from piracy and plunder to plantations and colonies in the sixteenth to eighteenth centuries.

▶ **Explore** how sugar and enslaved people became important in the Caribbean.

Why go to the Americas?

There were a number of reasons (or factors) why people chose to leave Britain for a new life in the New World.

Religious factors

In Britain, there were religious conflicts. Some religious groups such as Puritans and Catholics felt that they were not permitted to worship as they wished in Britain, so they left to settle in a place where they would have greater religious freedom. Find out more on pages 34–37.

Economic factors

Setting up colonies was not easy. Harsh weather and hunger were common, and settlers often came into conflict with **indigenous Americans** (also known as Native Americans), whose land they were occupying. However, following the establishment of the first successful British colony in America in 1607 (during the Stuart King James I's reign), more Britons were willing to settle in the New World as it became clear there was a lot of money to be made. There was plenty of land to grow new 'cash crops' such as cotton, tobacco, sugar and potatoes. These were grown on farms known as plantations and were exported back to Britain for great profit.

Into the Caribbean

It wasn't just North America where new colonies were set up. British businessmen (or traders) also set up plantations in the Caribbean on islands such as Bardados (1625) and the Cayman Islands (1670). Plantations

▼ **SOURCE A** *An illustration from 1590 showing English colonists approaching the island of Roanoke in 1585; it accompanied a report that tried to persuade others that there should be more British colonisation in North America*

soon grew in importance: as the Americas were so distant, the colonies depended on successful large-scale farming to survive.

Global trading

British investors were also keen on developing trade in the Americas, because it would help to pay for the growth of the British Empire elsewhere, in India. They realised that they could export crops such as cotton from the New World to Britain, while they could import and sell other goods to the colonies, such as wheat, rice and coffee. Also, the cotton from American plantations helped supply British fabric factories, which in return would sell the fabric to British colonies for further profit.

The British acquired Barbados from the Spanish in 1625. King Charles I then allowed the island to be established for tobacco plantations. To begin with, the older plantations in North America were more profitable than Barbados. However, by 1655, Barbados had become the largest British slave colony and was highly profitable. Plantations soon switched to growing sugar, and by the 1690s, most of the island was covered in successful sugar plantations. Barbados became far more profitable for the British than the mainland America colonies, mainly because it was seen as just a profit-making area, and not as a place to settle.

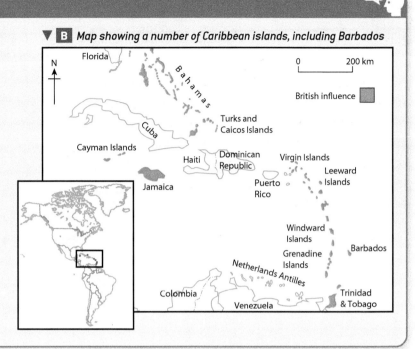

▼ **B** *Map showing a number of Caribbean islands, including Barbados*

Plantation replacing piracy

As Britain's worldwide empire grew in North America (and India), and became increasingly profitable, British monarchs stopped granting privateer permission because there was less need to steal from other nations. The Royal Navy also took increasingly effective anti-pirate measures. This meant that by the 1720s, piracy was rare in the Americas. Pirates were chased out of harbours where they had previously been able to seek safe haven, such as Nassau in the Bahamas. Plantations, not piracy, became the area where huge profits could be made for Britain.

The move to slavery

Many settlers soon found that conditions were hard on plantations: there were new diseases, the weather was too hot, and when crops failed, there was not always enough food for everyone. Not many people were willing to work the farms in these conditions, so the British began using **indentured servants** for labour. Indentured servants were people who paid for their voyage to America by being under contract to a plantation owner for a set period of years. At the end of this period they were then free to work for wages. However, by 1619, enslaved Africans were introduced to British plantations because they were cheaper: plantation owners could buy them outright. Enslaved people had no legal rights and had to work their whole lives without payment, and any children born became slave owners' property too. Purchasing enslaved people allowed plantations to become more profitable, as the unpaid workforce increased in size.

New World   plantation

indigenous American   indentured servant

The Spanish were the first to use enslaved people in the Americas. The British got involved with the slave trade in 1562, when Queen Elizabeth I gave John Hawkins permission to transport enslaved Africans to Spanish colonies. He took 300 Africans by force in Sierra Leone and traded them for goods such as sugar. He made a fortune.

1 Why did people leave Britain to settle in the New World?

2 Explain how the settlers hoped to make money in their new colonies.

3 How did the settlers find workers to establish and farm the crops they grew?

4 Why was slavery so profitable?

5 Study **Source A**. How useful is it to a historian studying the reasons for the British colonisation of North America?

The impact of the slave trade on Britain

From the 1560s, British merchants became involved in the slave trade, and in 1619, the first enslaved Africans arrived in the British colony of **Virginia** in America. In the 1700s alone, an estimated six million Africans were taken across the Atlantic Ocean to America and the Caribbean. Meanwhile, British slave traders made millions of pounds, making Britain one of the world's richest nations. How did the slave trade work, and what were the economic and cultural impacts of it on Britain?

Objectives

▶ **Outline** the development of the slave trade in the sixteenth and seventeenth centuries.

▶ **Explain** why the slave trade was so profitable.

▶ **Evaluate** the economic and social impact of the slave trade on Britain.

Slavery

The idea of slavery is very old, but enslaved people were used in very large numbers in the Tudor and Stuart periods, especially in the Americas. Enslaved people endured short and brutal lives of extreme misery: those on sugar plantations had an average life expectancy of 26, because they often had a poor diet, faced tough punishments and had no proper medical attention.

Development of the slave trade

Enslaved Africans were taken to the Americas and the Caribbean as a result of a three-part trading journey known as the **slave triangle**.

Traders made money from all parts of the slave triangle, earning up to 800 per cent profit. They just needed the initial investment to pay for the ship, a strong crew to

▼ **SOURCE B** *Formerly enslaved person Olaudah Equiano describes what enslaved people endured. At the time, the term 'negro' was used to describe black people, but it is considered offensive today.*

> I have seen a negro beaten till some of his bones were broken, for even letting a pot boil over.

control the enslaved people, and goods to trade for enslaved people on the African coast. Slave owners also profited: they forced enslaved people to work all their lives, without wages, and in great hardship. The increased slave trading up until the 1800s, and a growing slave population, meant that plantations became highly profitable. The growth of the British Empire also increased the demand for crops grown in plantations and the products made from them.

▼ **A** *The three parts of the slave triangle*

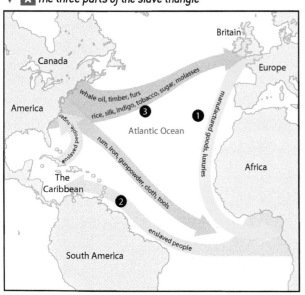

1 Traders leave Britain and other European ports, headed for Africa, with goods such as alcohol, guns and cloth.

2 Traders trade these goods with Africans in return for prisoners from other chiefdoms or kingdoms, who have been captured to sell; traders also kidnap Africans. Ships loaded with enslaved Africans sail across the Atlantic.

3 In the Americas, the enslaved Africans are traded to plantation owners and farmers for goods such as sugar, cotton or tobacco. These are shipped back to British or European ports to be sold at great profit.

SOURCE C *A painting (1823) by British artist William Clark, showing enslaved people cutting sugar cane in Antigua. Clark was invited there by slave owners, who may have hoped the painting would present a positive view of the slave trade at a time when many British people were calling for an end to slavery.*

Economic impact

Britain wasn't the only European nation to get involved in slavery during Tudor and Stuart times, but Britain made some of the largest profits. British slave traders didn't just work on their own either: they were supported by investors back in Britain, including monarchs. Although she found slavery 'detestable', Queen Elizabeth I was persuaded by the idea of great profits. She funded John Hawkins' second slave-trading voyage, giving British slave trading royal consent. King Charles II was a partner in the **Royal African Company**, a large slave-trading business that transported 60,000 enslaved people from Africa between 1680 and 1688. Many of the enslaved people were branded with the letters DY when they were captured, after the man who ran the company: James, Duke of York (the future King James II).

In fact, many Britons played a significant part in the slave trade – shipbuilders, ship owners (who allowed their ships to be used), bankers (who lent traders money), investors (who shared in the profits) and importers (who brought in the goods that enslaved people farmed). Many other Britons were linked in other ways: dockworkers unloading ships full of cotton that enslaved people had grown; workers turning the cotton into shirts; even the shop owners selling sugar and tobacco from the plantations. Whether directly or indirectly, all these people gained financially from slave trading: the British slave trade industry made approximately £60 million between 1761 and 1808, making Britain one of the richest and most powerful nations in the world.

Key Words

Virginia   slave triangle
Royal African Company   Maroons

Social impact

During the eighteenth century, Glasgow and Bristol grew into large cities as they benefited from the shipping trade. Many of the fine buildings in these places (and some in London) were paid for with the profits of slavery. A large number of Liverpool's mayors were slave traders and so were many MPs in parliament.

SOURCE D *George F. Cooke, a well-known British actor, said the following in 1785:*

> Every brick in the city of Liverpool is cemented with the blood of a slave.

Before the 1800s, it was not illegal to make money from slave trading. And because the trade was so widespread, and involved so many British people in power, the belief grew that Europeans were superior to Africans. However, enslaved people had been rebelling for years – for example, the Jamaican **Maroons**, who escaped their plantations in 1655. Some people in Britain now also felt slavery was wrong, and by the late 1700s a campaign for its abolition had started. In 1807, the British parliament abolished the slave trade, and by 1833, it banned slave ownership throughout the British Empire. However, in 1833 the government agreed to pay £20 million to former slave owners for their 'loss of property'. For example, the Bishop of Exeter received over £12,000 for the loss of 665 slaves.

Work

1 Describe how the slave trade developed in the sixteenth and seventeenth centuries.

2 List the ways Britain was linked to the slave trade.

Practice Question

Explain two ways in which the Vikings and the British slave traders were similar.   **8 marks**

British colonies in America

In the sixteenth and early seventeenth centuries, people began to leave different European countries and settle in America. Early British settlers occupied the east coast of North America. These British settlements, or colonies, made up what could be described as Britain's first successful overseas empire. By the mid-1700s there were 13 successful British colonies. Who were the early settlers, and why did they leave Britain? What were the consequences of British colonisation for the indigenous peoples of America?

Objectives

▶ **Identify** different causes of British migration to North America.

▶ **Examine** the roles of Sir Walter Raleigh and the Pilgrim Fathers in establishing early colonies such as Jamestown.

▶ **Assess** the impact of the arrival of the British on indigenous people.

Why did people leave Britain?

Several causes made people leave Britain at this time. Firstly, economic problems meant that unemployment among farmhands and labourers was high, and wages were low. People struggled to survive, and sometimes faced starvation as a result of failed harvests. As a result, a new start in a new land seemed very appealing.

Secondly, some Christian groups, such as **Puritans**, **Quakers** and **Catholics**, had suffered **persecution** in Britain since the 1530s, when King Henry VIII turned the country from Catholic to **Protestant**. For example, failure to attend **Anglican** Church services was punishable by prison or even execution. As a result, many of these religious groups left Britain to settle in North America, where they set up or joined colonies. Around 80,000 Puritans migrated to America between 1630 and 1641.

Emigration peaked during the **Civil Wars** and the time of Oliver Cromwell's rule in Britain (1642–60), partly due to the fact that

differences in religious beliefs led to conflicts between religious groups. Furthermore, religious groups in mainland Europe also wanted to escape persecution: some Dutch, French and Germans emigrated from the 1560s onwards. Some religious groups also wanted to emigrate in order to convert the indigenous Americans to Christianity.

▼ **A** *The 13 American colonies, the goods and crops they produced, and early British settlements*

What was attractive about North America?

People from overcrowded British towns were excited by the vast expanse of new land available in America, and by the chance to make money. Settlers grew crops such as tobacco, corn and cotton, and then transported these **commodities** back to Britain to sell. Livestock sales were also successful. This drove British businessmen to invest in more voyages. North American seas were stocked with profitable cod, and by the late 1600s, sugar plantations were also bringing in huge profits for Britain.

Early settlers and colonies

Life for the early British settlers in the colonies was not easy to begin with, however. They often faced hardship and failure. Two case studies – Virginia and Massachusetts – highlight how settlers tried to establish colonies.

Extension

Sir Walter Raleigh was in the top 100 'Greatest Britons' in a poll among British people in 2002. Research Raleigh further and explain whether you agree with the title of 'Father of American Colonies', even though those colonies failed.

Case study: Virginia

In the late 1500s, many British people tried to establish settlements in the area known as Virginia, but they failed to survive. In 1606, King James I gave permission for a group of businessmen to sail to Virginia, to establish a new colony called **Jamestown**, to see if the land was fit to grow crops, and to find gold if possible. The colony was founded in 1607. There was some conflict between the early settlers and the indigenous Americans whose land they were occupying. However, the settlers had to rely on local indigenous people to help them find and grow food – particularly as some of the early settlers were wealthy aristocrats who were unused to doing farm work. Life in Jamestown meant hunger and death for many, but the settlers were determined to stay. With the support of some indigenous people, the settlers began to farm the land successfully, rather than focus on the search for gold. Tobacco planting in particular led to the success of Jamestown: tobacco was easy to grow and made high profits. This led to more and more British **migrants** seeking their fortune in the New World. Other settlements such as New Plymouth soon sprung up along the east coast of America – eventually developing into **13 colonies**.

Key Words

Puritan Quaker Catholic persecution Protestant Anglican civil war commodity Jamestown migrant   13 colonies

Work

1 a List the reasons why Britons migrated to, and built colonies in, North America.
   b Which reason do you think is the most important one? Why?
2 Why did the Jamestown settlers succeed?
3 Describe what Sir Walter Raleigh did to help Britain colonise North America.

Practice Question

Was religion the main factor in causing migration to America?

| **16 marks** |
| **SPaG: 4 marks** |

Study Tip

For 'main factor' questions you will need to explain how religion and other factors caused migration (see Chapters 5 and 6). Was religion or another cause the main factor?

Key Biography

Sir Walter Raleigh (c1554–1618)

Sir Walter Raleigh was a sea captain for both Queen Elizabeth I and her successor King James I. In 1584, the queen sent him to start settlements in Virginia. These early colonies faced numerous problems: the settlers were frequently short on supplies, they struggled to grow crops, there were attacks from indigenous Americans, and they caught diseases like malaria. However, Raleigh is known as the 'Father of American Colonies' for establishing colonies such as Roanoke (in 1584).

British colonies in America

Case study: Massachusetts

One of the most famous groups of British people to settle in America arrived in 1620 on a ship called the *Mayflower*. They were mainly Puritans; strict Protestant Christians who left because they were persecuted by others who did not agree with their religious beliefs. They, and other settlers, set up their own religious colony known as 'New Plymouth', with the aim of fishing and trading with other colonies. Enough of the colonists survived the winter, with help from local indigenous people, for it to become the first permanent colony (Jamestown eventually became deserted). These settlers became known as the **Pilgrim Fathers**.

▼ **INTERPRETATION B** *A nineteenth-century painting showing the Puritans arriving in America in 1620, with the* Mayflower *sailing away into the distance*

The New Plymouth colony worked very hard, and offshore fishing became the main source of farming: cod was in high demand as one of the few highly nutritious foods in British diets at this time. The settlers wanted peace and order in the colony, so they quickly established **democratic** principles and a **constitution**, to ensure that their Puritan religious beliefs would remain central to colony life. The example of the Pilgrim Fathers led to more religious groups moving to this area: more than 20,000 settlers arrived in Massachusetts between 1629 and 1640. The Pilgrim Fathers weren't just British **emigrants** looking for quick wealth.

In fact, they managed to create religious and democratic rules and traditions that would become the foundation of modern America.

▼ **SOURCE C** *Chief Powhatan, leader of the Powhatan chiefdom, said the following to the settler Captain John Smith in the early 1600s:*

> Your coming is not for trade, but to invade my people and possess my country.

Impact of British colonies on indigenous Americans

The indigenous people in America had been there long before any Europeans. There were many communities, with different cultures. Most did not have permanent settlements: they lived off the land and established camps where appropriate. As such, the British arrival in North America could be interpreted in different ways. For example, indigenous Americans would have seen the British as invaders, who took territory by force and wiped out several communities by passing on diseases that their immune systems could not deal with.

As in Jamestown and New Plymouth, early settlers' relations with the indigenous Americans were varied. Good relations initially existed with indigenous chiefdoms such as the Powhatan, and there were some intermarriages. However, in general, the British did not treat them with respect. Massacres were carried out on both sides, over land claims, but some settlers were particularly vicious: they often attacked and destroyed indigenous people's crops and villages. In 1500, there were approximately 560,000 indigenous Americans in 'British' territories. However, by 1700, there were fewer than 280,000. Devastating European diseases such as measles and smallpox, the ill treatment of indigenous American people, and British expansion into indigenous territory all had a huge impact on indigenous Americans. Many had to find a new way of life, adapt to European ways,

SOURCE D *A seventeenth-century drawing of Captain John Smith's encounter with indigenous people in Virginia; Smith was a well-known early British settler who became internationally famous when Disney animated the story of Pocahontas; the drawing appeared in a book published in 1624 by Captain Smith, called The Generall Historie of Virginia, New-England, and the Summer Isles*

How they tooke him prifoner in the Oaze 1607.

C.Smith bindeth a faluage to his arme fighteth with the King of Pamaunkee and all his company, and flew 3 of them.

or move further inland to avoid the settlers. Today, indigenous Americans account for only 0.7 per cent of the total population of the USA.

For the British settlers, however, overall they gained a better life in the 13 colonies, and saw it as a land of opportunity and freedom where British culture and religious beliefs could thrive.

SOURCE E *Adapted from a description of the indigenous people encountered by the Virginian settlers, from the document* Nova Britannia, *written in 1609:*

> It is inhabited by wild and savage people that live all over the forests. They have no law but native. They are easy to be brought to good [Christian ways] but would happily like better conditions.

Work

1 Describe the successes of the Pilgrim Fathers.

2 Identify the advantages and disadvantages about colonisation of North America to: the British; the indigenous American people.

3 a Study **Source D**. What is happening in the drawing?
   b Compare **Source D** and **Source E**. Explain how they are similar in their attitudes to indigenous Americans.

4 What was the British attitude to indigenous Americans in the sixteenth and seventeenth centuries? Explain your answer.

Practice Question

How useful is **Source D** to a historian studying the impact on the indigenous peoples of the British colonisation of North America?   **8 marks**

Study Tip

Use the information about the provenance of the source, as well as what you can see in the image, in your answer.

5.2 Why did the British fall out with the American colonists?

By the 1760s, the British had gained an overseas empire in North America. They controlled a huge area of land on the eastern coast, stretching back from the Atlantic Ocean to the Mississippi River. Divided into 13 colonies, each had strong ties to Britain. But in 1776, these 13 colonies broke away from Britain and declared themselves to be united as one independent country – the United States of America. How and why did this happen?

Objective

▶ **Define** the Navigation Acts, the Stamp Act and the Boston Tea Party.

▶ **Identify** factors that led to American discontentment with Britain.

▶ **Categorise** reasons why Americans wanted independence from Britain.

Independent minds

The people who lived in the British colonies of North America by the 1760s were tough and independently minded. Many of them descended from the early Puritans and Quakers who had gone to America to escape religious persecution, or because they were unhappy with the British monarch. During the British Civil Wars in the mid-seventeenth century, Britain did not really have time to deal with the overseas colonies, which meant the people there got used to not having the British intervene with their way of life. The colonies successfully traded products such as bread, clothing, books and guns with each other. Indentured servants and enslaved people could be bought and sold too, and human trade became a profitable industry. All this meant the colonies had a strong economy that didn't rely on trade with Britain. Before long, there were ideas among the colonists that they could exist separately from Britain.

Independent actions

In Virginia and other colonies, the British idea of having a class system of aristocrats (titled nobles) and monarchs was seen as outdated. The colonists who had succeeded in America were 'self-made' businessmen. Even though most had made their fortunes from plantations and the slave trade they were built on, many of these colonists believed that anyone could make a success of themselves, no matter what their background. Early colonies such as New Plymouth also set up their own constitutions, which clashed with British rule. So the idea of being governed by men far away in Britain, who had inherited their wealth, started to seem odd. Over time, they began to dislike the control of their colonies by the British, and did not want to be a part of the British Empire. Some negative attitudes towards colonists by the people in Britain didn't help either.

▼ **SOURCE A** *Adapted from a document called 'On the Plantation Trade', written in 1698 by an English economist and politician who recommended government control of colonial economies:*

> That our subjects in the American colonies are children of the state, and are to be treated as such, no one denies; but it can't reasonably be admitted that the mother country should [ruin] herself to enrich the children, nor that Great Britain should weaken herself to strengthen America.

The Navigation Acts

When the British started to intervene too much in American affairs it caused resentment among the colonists. The **Navigation Acts** of 1651–73 contributed to the colonists' desire for independence from Britain. These acts were introduced to enrich Britain; they were a series of laws which stipulated that American colonies could only import (buy) and export (sell) goods with British ships sailing to and from British ports. This **monopoly** of trade with just the British greatly restricted the type and amount of goods that could be brought to America, which meant competition for products was scarce, and so prices were often very high. When American colonists tried to smuggle in cheaper goods from other countries, the British patrolled the waters and seized the smugglers.

Taxation

If the colonists wanted to buy anything from countries other than Britain, the goods had to go first to Britain, where they were taxed. There was a very high tax on goods such as glass, coffee, wine and sugar. There was also the **Stamp Act** of 1765, which imposed a tax on the paper used for official documents. Colonists were also made to pay taxes to fund the British wars against the French that the colonists felt had little to do with them. Some colonists started to believe that if they were taxed so heavily, then they should have representatives in the British parliament, and have a say in British government.

▼ **SOURCE B** The Colonies Reduced *was published in Britain in 1767; it appeared in colonial newspapers as a protest against the hated Stamp Act. The cartoon depicts Britannia, and she is surrounded by her amputated limbs which are named Virginia, Pennsylvania, New York and New England.*

Key Words

Navigation Acts   monopoly
Stamp Act   Boston Tea Party

The Boston Tea Party

Colonists had many reasons to complain, and so a conflict began to build. Colonists were especially upset when the British taxed tea: three pence was paid to Britain for every pound of tea sold in America. In protest, a group of Americans boarded British ships in Boston, in December 1773, and dumped 342 crates full of tea (worth around £11,000) into the harbour. The British responded to the '**Boston Tea Party**' by closing Boston port, causing even more anger. When the British also banned all town meetings, the Americans began meeting in secret. In 1774, 56 representatives from the colonies met in Philadelphia to decide what to do. This meeting is known as the 'First Congress' (and even today, the American parliament is still known as Congress). Delegates at the First Congress decided to fight the British: the War of Independence began.

Extension

Research the First Congress of 1774 further to find out who attended and what they agreed. Which of the 13 colonies did not send a representative? Why?

Practice Question

Study **Source B**. How useful is it to a historian studying British involvement in America in the eighteenth century?   **8 marks**

Study Tip

Explain the point the cartoonist is making about the consequences of enforcing the Stamp Act.

Work

1 List the reasons why Americans wanted independence from Britain, and how they achieved it. Try to categorise your reasons into 'long-term causes' and 'short-term causes'.

2 Create a timeline of what happened in American and British relations, with the following dates: mid-seventeenth century, 1765, 1773, 1774.

What did losing the American colonies 'cost'?

When discussing the history of the British Empire, historians often mention the 'rise and fall of the British Empire'. The loss of the American colonies at the Treaty of Paris (1783) was certainly a setback. But was it a complete failure for Britain?

Objectives

▶ **Describe** what happened in the American War of Independence.

▶ **Explain** why it happened.

▶ **Analyse** the results of losing the American colonies.

The War of Independence

The British sent soldiers to force the American rebels to stay loyal, but they were met with fierce resistance. In July 1775, the Americans appointed George Washington as the leader of their army – he would go on to become their first President. A year later, in July 1776, Congress met again and formally declared themselves independent from Britain.

▼ **SOURCE A** *A nineteenth century painting showing the surrender of the British (in red) to the Americans (in blue)*

Although the 13 American colonies declared independence in 1776, there was over five years of bitter fighting before the British conceded that they had lost. War officially ended on 3 September 1783, when the Treaty of Paris was signed; but it is the British surrender at the Battle of Yorktown (1781) that was seen as the decisive end of the war. Britain had lost many battles throughout the war, but Yorktown was the most humiliating because the Americans completely surrounded the British and forced

Lord Cornwallis, Britain's army leader, to surrender. After Yorktown, Britain realised that victory was impossible and America's ally, the French, increased their support for the Americans further. This meant Britain had little choice but to formally sign the Treaty of Paris, and so this valuable colony was lost to Britain.

Losing America, gaining an empire?

The maps on these pages help us understand the consequences, for Britain and its empire, of losing the American colonies.

▼ **B** *The British Empire in 1775*

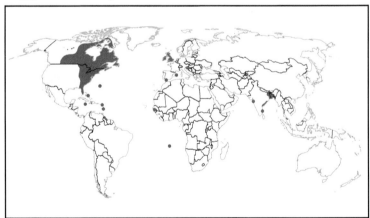

Canada

When America broke away from British rule in 1776, the colonies to the north (now known as Canada) remained part of the British Empire. These huge colonies, such as Quebec, Ontario, New Brunswick and Nova Scotia, remained a key part of the empire for nearly a century, until they achieved 'self-government' (the right to run most of their own affairs) in 1867. America lost 100,000 settlers to Canada, who preferred to emigrate rather than live under a republican government.

Britain

The war cost an estimated £80 million, which increased Britain's debts. However, Britain was rapidly industrialising and was very wealthy. But the human costs were high, with an estimated 10,000 British soldiers dying during battles or from disease, and up to about 20,000 sailors dying.

Britain and America were soon trading again after the war, and by 1785 this trade was back to its pre-war levels. For example, the British slave trade to the Americas continued. As the USA eventually became an ally of Britain's, losing it was not important in the long term. Britain's pride may have been dented, but financially, Britain was still as strong as before – if not more. Since the age of Elizabethan exploration, Britain had had a very strong navy, and by 1813 it had developed into the world's biggest. It helped to defend Britain's existing colonies, gain new colonies, and fight against opponents such as the French. The British Empire stretched from Canada to the Caribbean, parts of Africa (see Chapter 8), and India (see Chapter 7), and Britain was able to focus its wealth and resources in expanding and developing these. The vast territories gained in Africa and India between the 1700s and 1920 meant that Britain controlled a quarter of the world. At that point, the British Empire was the biggest empire the world had ever known.

Key Word

republic

The Caribbean and South America

Britain colonised parts of the Caribbean and the eastern coast of North America from the 1500s, until American independence in 1776. After that, Britain kept Central American territories (and Canada) until the nineteenth and twentieth centuries. Central American areas such as Anguilla, Montserrat and the Cayman Islands, as well as the Falkland Islands in South America, are examples of countries in the Americas that remained a part of the British Empire.

▼ **C** *The British Empire in 1920*

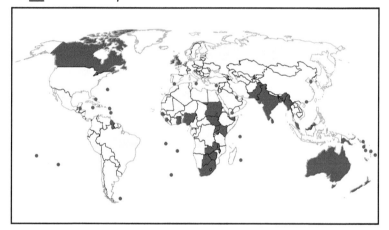

Australia

After the War of Independence, Britain needed a new place to send criminals, because it was no longer able to send them to America. Australia became the place to send them. Furthermore, like New Zealand and Canada, Australia was a loyal and dutiful colony. It provided willing markets for British goods, and also locations for ambitious or poverty-stricken Britons to emigrate to.

The USA

After beating the British, America was now a **republic** controlling its own political and economic affairs. It was now free to develop and expand as it wished. However, America lost up to 25,000 men during the war, mostly through disease. The impact of the soldiers' deaths on American labour and industry was felt for many years. On the other hand, the result of the war meant that Americans were able to forge stronger links with the French, since they had supported the Americans against the British. However, the cost of helping the Americans fight caused severe problems in France, which developed into their own revolution – the French Revolution – in 1789.

Work

1. Identify three consequences of Britain losing the American War of Independence.

2. Write a short paragraph explaining what you think is the significance of the War of Independence for Britain.

3. Were political or economic reasons responsible for causing the War of Independence in 1775? Explain your answer.

The first 'refugees': Huguenot migration

While some British people headed to America between the sixteenth and eighteenth centuries, people from other countries migrated to Britain. Immigrants who were escaping religious persecution from France, for example, contributed greatly to British life at this time. However, their migration provoked anti-French and anti-immigration feelings. Were these French Protestants, known as Huguenots, a welcome addition to Britain?

Objectives

▶ **Identify** the reasons Huguenots emigrated to Britain between the 1500s and the 1700s.

▶ **Explore** the consequences of Huguenot migration to Britain.

French Protestants arrive in Britain

France was a Catholic country, but it experienced a series of religious civil wars between the 1560s and the 1590s. The ruling French Catholics severely persecuted those who wanted to follow Protestantism. Hostilities reached a peak in August 1572 when tens of thousands of French Protestants were killed in the St Bartholomew's Day Massacre. To escape the killings, French Protestants (or Huguenots) started to emigrate to many different destinations, and neighbouring Britain was an ideal choice. This was because England's King Henry VIII had turned the country from Catholic to Protestant during the English **Reformation** in the 1530s.

French emigration continued when Henry's Protestant children, Edward VI and Elizabeth I, ruled England. They made the country a welcome place of refuge for fellow Protestants. Edward VI, for example, allowed the first French church to be set up, and Elizabeth's ministers invited skilled Huguenot craftspeople to work in England and teach British apprentices their skills. As some Huguenots settled in Britain, more from abroad followed them. Indeed, from Elizabeth's time onwards, Britain experienced an ongoing boom in wealth as the first industrialised nation, and skilled Huguenots played a part in this.

Fact

St Bartholomew's Day Massacre

An estimated 3000 Protestants were murdered in Paris in this massacre in August 1572, and as many as 70,000 throughout France. The massacre started because Catholics believed Protestants were plotting rebellions and war with Spain. This event marked a turning point in the French religious wars, and the Huguenots lost many of their leaders.

Another period of migration

The number of French migrants fleeing to Britain began to drop as the French religious wars ended by 1598. French King Henri IV issued a bill of rights for the Huguenots called the **Edict of Nantes**, which granted them freedom to practise their religion without fear. However, France became an unwelcome and dangerous place for French Protestants again in the time of Henri's grandson, King Louis XIV. He agreed with his advisers that allowing Huguenots to remain in France meant a threat to his own absolute power as king. He withdrew the privileges Huguenots had been granted since his grandfather's time, and gave Protestant ministers the choice of converting to Catholicism or emigrating. Protestant families faced increasing intimidation. In 1685, Louis tore up the Edict of Nantes: without this written legal protection, the Huguenots were officially **heretics** and faced persecution once more. This time, despite a ban on fleeing the country, up to 200,000 Huguenots fled from France. Many faced risky journeys at sea, including up to 50,000 who escaped to England.

▼ **SOURCE A** *A drawing, from 1685, of French Huguenots landing at Dover, fleeing from France when Louis XIV revoked the Edict of Nantes*

Impact of the Huguenots in Britain

The French Huguenots contributed much to British life and had a positive social and economic impact on Britain. As they were largely highly skilled craftsmen and women, they revitalised British industries such as watch-making, gun-making and bookbinding. Huguenot weavers, merchants and joiners established businesses in communities as far apart as London, Plymouth, Rochester, Norwich and Canterbury.

▼ **SOURCE B** *A painting by Hogarth, from 1738, showing Huguenots (on the right) attending a church in London; on the left are Londoners. Hogarth was a famous English painter who used art to critique society and politics of the time.*

The Huguenots transformed existing British industries, and started up new ones such as paper-making. With no paper mills before the Huguenots arrived, Britain's paper industry relied mainly on imports from France. But by the 1710s, Huguenot expertise meant that Britain boasted 200 paper mills, supplying nearly 70 per cent of Britain's paper market. British banknotes were printed by a Huguenot business from 1712 onwards, for over 250 years. Britain also gained scientists, intellectuals and experts from France that boosted the country's business, arts and crafts.

However, there was some anti-Huguenot feeling in Britain upon their arrival. Some felt that they took jobs away from English people and were full of diseases. They ate strange foods (such as snails) and one Bristol MP even compared them to one of the plagues of Egypt in the Bible. But, in time, the Huguenots merged into English society. They changed or translated their surnames to

sound more English (Blanc became White, for example) and married English men and women.

The impact of the Huguenot migration was significant for France too: France lost many talented merchants and craftsmen and women. Its glassware and hat-making industries were lost, for example. In fact, France was so badly affected that King Louis XIV's ambassador to Britain offered Huguenots cash to return to France! The Huguenots were France's loss and Britain's gain.

Work

1   How useful is **Source B** to a historian studying British attitudes towards immigrants to Britain in the 1700s? Explain your answer using **Source B** and your contextual knowledge.

2   Has religion been the main factor in causing migration to and from Britain since 790? Explain your answer with reference to religion and other factors. Look back over your notes from previous chapters to refresh your memory.

Extension

Conduct research to find out more about the impact of Huguenots migrating to cities in Britain. For example, look at the website www.huguenotsofspitalfields.org. What effects have the Huguenots had on London by living in areas like Spitalfields or Soho?

Practice Question

Explain two ways in which the impact of the Huguenots on Britain and the Pilgrim Fathers on America were similar.   **8 marks**

Study Tip

You will need to refresh yourself with the events of the Pilgrim Fathers migrating to America in Chapter 5. To work out the similarities, you could consider making a list of categories to compare with, such as timescale of the migrations, causes for migration, numbers, locations, and consequences for Britain.

What were the Ulster Plantations and the Highland Clearances?

6.2

While Huguenots were moving into Britain, there was also a great movement of people out of, and around, the country. In the northern part of Ireland (known as Ulster), English and Scottish Protestants settled on land confiscated from the Irish, while people who lived in the Highlands of Scotland moved to the Scottish Lowlands and other parts of Britain, or emigrated abroad.

Objectives

▶ **Define** the Ulster Plantations and the Highland Clearances.

▶ **Explain** the background to these events.

▶ **Analyse** the impact of Scottish migration to England and emigration abroad.

The Ulster Plantations

The **Ulster Plantations** began in the early 1600s during the reign of King James I of England (and VI of Scotland). He 'planted' the northern part of Ireland (Ulster) with Protestants from Scotland and England, hoping they would be obedient to him and his government. Most settlers moved hoping to find a new and better life for themselves and their families, but most Irish people resented what they saw as an 'invasion'.

The Ulster Plantations brought big changes. The population grew rapidly as thousands of settlers arrived, and they brought with them new customs and a new religion – Protestantism. Resentment between the Protestant settlers and the mainly Catholic Irish continued for centuries and often spilled over into violence.

▼ **A** *The Ulster Plantations; the settlers were given the name 'undertakers', because they had to undertake certain conditions, including building a house and 'bawn' (fortified barn), and to settle the land with a minimum number of people of the Protestant faith*

The Highland Clearances

In the early 1700s, over half the people in Scotland lived in the Highlands. Most spoke Gaelic, a language similar to Irish, and the way of life was different from those who lived in Lowland Scotland. Many Highlanders belonged to 'clans' (a type of 'family group'). Clan members supported their chief in return for protection and leadership. Most Highlanders were farmers, and families lived on the same small farms for generations. They lived in simple stone cottages called crofts, and made money from selling wheat they grew on the farms. In the Lowlands, the towns and cities were growing, and manufacturers and merchants were becoming wealthy.

The Highlanders were largely Catholics and Jacobites (supporters of the Stuart royal family), and had participated in the Stuart-led **Jacobite Rebellions**. These occurred in 1715 and 1745–46 after the last Stuart monarch, Queen Anne, died in 1714 and the German prince George of Hanover took over as King George I. Descendants of the Stuarts tried to regain the throne through the rebellions, but they failed. After they had been finally defeated at the Battle of Culloden in 1746, the English wanted to reduce the power of the Highlanders, since many of them were loyal to the Stuarts, and not to George I.

The English began a brutal policy of removing all potential opposition in the Highlands by eliminating Scottish chiefs who supported the Stuarts, together with their clans. Some chiefs had no choice but to keep the English happy; they did this by supporting English demands to clear the Highlands of its clans, in what became known as the **Highland Clearances**. Laws were passed making life difficult for Highlanders, and bagpipes were banned because they were viewed as 'instruments of war'.

A new type of farming in the Highlands

Much of the land in the Highlands was owned by Englishmen and rented by Highlanders. However, at this time, the English landlords began to prefer the idea of having large sheep farms, rather than renting small strips of land to tenant farming families. Sheep farming made the landlords more money. However, the Highland farmers were usually too poor to buy the large numbers of sheep needed, so chiefs and landlords began to clear the Highlanders away to make way for the more profitable sheep farming. Many were forced to move to towns and cities in the Lowlands to look for work, but many more emigrated abroad.

▼ **SOURCE B** *A painting by Scottish artist Thomas Faed, called* The Last of the Clan *(1865); Faed was a popular and respected artist in London; the women in the picture are fashionably dressed for peasants*

How were the Highlands cleared?

Different tactics were used to clear the Highlands. From the 1780s to the 1820s, tens of thousands of Highlanders were evicted from their homes. Evictions of up to 2000 families in one day were not uncommon. Highland families were forced onto barren coastal land, or other unworkable land, and many starved to death. Highlanders who refused to leave could be killed. Even the old and dying had their homes burned or were thrown out in the open to die. Many of the chiefs were fully aware of what was going on; and many clans felt betrayed.

Impact on the British Empire

Thousands of Scottish people emigrated during the era of the Highland Clearances, to countries such as Canada, America and England as well as to Scottish cities such as Dundee, Edinburgh and Glasgow.

The word **diaspora** describes the scattering of a group of people across a wide location. The Scottish diaspora contributed greatly to those countries in which the Highlanders settled – and to the empire itself. Many Scots contributed engineering skills to the building of roads, railways and many building schemes in the colonies. Many of the empire's greatest explorers, such as David Livingstone, were Scottish. Some historians argue that the empire didn't really start expanding until England and Scotland stopped fighting and the Scots put their efforts into empire-building. The British Empire was most certainly British, not English.

How and why did Britain gain control of India?

India today is an independent country in Asia. It's the second most populated country in the world. Over thousands of years, people from all over the world have settled in India, or tried to conquer it. The Persians and Iranians settled there in ancient times. Famous conquerors such as Genghis Khan invaded it – and so did Alexander the Great. The Chinese came to India in pursuit of knowledge and to visit the ancient Indian universities. And then came the French, the Dutch, and finally the British.

Objectives

▶ **Define** how trade in Indian goods worked in the seventeenth and eighteenth centuries.

▶ **Explore** who Britain competed with for a hold over India, including the East India Company, Robert Clive and Warren Hastings.

▶ **Evaluate** how important India was economically to Britain's empire.

Why did India appeal to European traders?

India is rich in natural resources – iron ore, silk, copper, gold, silver, gemstones, tea and timber. Spices (which were very valuable in the Middle Ages) are common in India too. This meant that any country that made strong trade links with India could potentially become very rich and powerful.

▼ SOURCE A *A British trading station in Bombay (now known as Mumbai) in the 1750s*

Rivalry among nations

In 1497, a Portuguese explorer named Vasco De Gama discovered how to get to India from Europe by sea. Soon many European countries (including Denmark, France and the Netherlands) were sending ships to India to trade. At first the ships simply reached an Indian port and bartered with local traders, swapping items such as guns, swords, buttons or shoes for silk, spices, cotton or tea. The European traders then brought these back to their own countries to sell for a big profit.

Fact

India became a valuable source of people – as well as spices, tea and cotton. As a small island, Britain could not always find enough people to help control its growing empire. So, the British created a system to train and pay local Indian people to become soldiers and fight for them. As a result, huge numbers of Indians became the fighting force of the country that had colonised them. In years to come, Indian soldiers would play a significant role in both world wars.

With the permission of local Indian rulers, the European traders began to set up more permanent bases along the Indian coast. Known as **trading stations**, these large warehouses were surrounded by huge walls and guarded by men with guns. The goods were stored in the warehouses and this was where the trading took place. Sometimes the traders lived there with their families too. There were often workshops or 'factories' within these trading ports that turned some of the raw materials into goods. Cotton cloth, for example, was woven by Indian weavers and exported by the British in huge quantities to supply the demand for cheap, washable, lightweight fabric. Opium, an addictive drug, was also grown and sold by British traders in China at a huge profit.

The East India Company

In the early years of European trade with India, the main countries with trading stations were France, the Netherlands and Britain. The British trading stations were run by one company – the East India Company (EIC). It had been trading all over the world since it was set up in 1600. The company's ships carried cheap British goods and exchanged them for goods in countries as far away as Japan and China. They then brought the fine china, silk, coffee and spices back to Britain. As a result, India became a base for some of Britain's growing global trading, and became increasingly important. The businessmen in charge of the company, and the kings and queens to whom they paid taxes, made a fortune from this trade.

The East India Company first set up trading posts in India in Surat (1612), Madras (1638) and Bombay (1668). It had a monopoly in British trade in India to begin with, but this ended in 1694. However, by then the EIC was so powerful, with its own army and navy, that it continued to be the major force in trade in India for the next century.

Practice Question

Explain two ways in which British actions in India and those in North America in the seventeenth century were different.   **8 marks**

Key Word

trading station

▼ **B** *A map of India and the main trading stations, showing the countries that ran them*

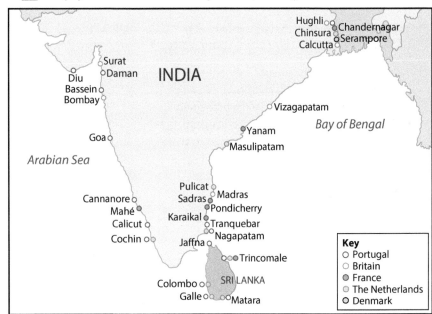

Work

1 Why do you think European nations took such an interest in India?
2 Look at **Source A** and map **B**.
   a What is a trading station?
   b List the countries that set up trading stations in India in the 1600s.
3 What was the East India Company?
4 Explain how the East India Company made such huge profits from trading in India. You could present your ideas as a diagram, poster or leaflet.

Extension

Research the history of the East India Company. When was it formed, and by whom? What goods did it trade in most often? How successful was it? Did it trade in places other than India? What happened to the company?

Study Tip

Consider how India and North America were different at that time.

How and why did Britain gain control of India?

Control in India during early European exploration and trade

Before the 1500s, the Indian subcontinent was divided into lots of kingdoms. Most were run by Hindu princes. These kingdoms would occasionally go to war against each other – but they largely witnessed long, peaceful periods. However, in the early 1500s, the Mughals (who were Muslims) invaded India and took control. Within decades, the great Mughal Emperor Akbar had managed to unite many of the Indian states and ruled over all the Hindu princes.

For the most part, the next few generations of Mughal Emperors ruled peacefully. However, Akbar's great-grandson, Aurangzeb, was a fanatical Muslim and persecuted followers of India's other religions. Wars broke out all over India during the reign of Aurangzeb (1658–1707), and the Mughals began to lose control of the country by the late 1600s and early 1700s. It was at exactly this time, when much of India was at war, that some European nations – and powerful trading companies such as the East India Company – began to take advantage of the situation.

European invasion in the seventeenth and eighteenth centuries

Control over the goods coming out of India wasn't the only thing that attracted the Europeans: India was a good place in which to sell their own goods to the many millions of Indians in their territory. Furthermore, Dutch, French and British companies realised that by helping certain Hindu princes (by providing them with weapons and soldiers, for example), they could affect the outcome of the wars, and help the princes to beat their enemies. They could then demand rewards from the princes they had supported – perhaps land or goods. Furthermore, if they ever fell out with a prince, and fought against him, they could win and take his territory!

The East India Company expands

In the 1700s, the EIC began to take more and more Indian land. It had its own private army and navy, and used them against various regional rulers of India. For example, at the Battle of Plassey in 1757, around 3000 company troops (2200 of whom were local Indians) led by Robert Clive defeated an Indian army of over 40,000, led by local prince Siraj-ud-Daula (who was helped by the French). This allowed the EIC to take over Bengal, one of the richest parts of India formally ruled by Siraj-ud-Daula. The company also fought against other European nations, such as the Dutch, and took over their trading posts.

Key Biography

Robert Clive (1725–74)
- Started work as an EIC office clerk aged 18.
- Joined the EIC's army and proved an effective and ruthless military leader.
- While Governor of Bengal, won the Battle of Plassey in 1757 and oversaw plunder of the region, making a personal fortune.
- Back in England, was elected to parliament in 1761 and knighted in 1764.
- Returned to India as Governor and Commander-in-Chief of Bengal 1764–67. His greed and mismanagement increased the devastation of the 1700 Bengal famine, in which about ten million died.
- Criticised by parliament in 1772 for corruption.

▼ **INTERPRETATION C** *A c.1900 image of the Battle of Plassey in June 1757; Colonel Robert Clive's portrait is at top left.*

Over the following decades, more and more of India came under the rule of the East India Company. However, despite making huge profits in India, the EIC was losing money elsewhere, mainly as a result of a decline in trade with America at this time. So the British government decided to step in and help out with the company's financial problems. After all, the government didn't want this British company (which paid a fortune in taxes) to go bankrupt and lose control of large parts of India. So in 1773, the Government of India Act stated that both the British government and the East India Company controlled the territory in India jointly. A Governor General was appointed to control the territory, and Warren Hastings was given the job.

After Britain lost the valuable American colonies in the late 1700s (see pages 38–41), India became an even more important part of the empire. The British government became increasingly involved in India and gradually took more control of the EIC's affairs. By the mid-1850s, much of India was controlled by the British, but a major rebellion, one that would shock the world, was just around the corner.

Key Biography

Warren Hastings (1732–1818)

- First Governor General of India (1774–85).
- Strengthened British control in India, helping to establish India as part of the British Empire.
- Introduced many reforms including remodelling the administration, reorganising tax systems, tightening anti-corruption laws, and wiping out thieving gangs who were running wild in the countryside.
- Faced accusations of corruption, mismanagement and poor military judgement from political rivals.
- Back in England, faced trial in 1787 over concerns about British standards in India. He was found not guilty in 1795.

▼ **INTERPRETATION D** *Adapted from* The British Empire, 1815–1914 *by Frank McDonough:*

> Robert Clive, who became known later as 'Clive of India', brought Calcutta and Bengal under the control of the company, negotiated important trade agreements with the numerous independent regional princes, pushed the French out of India, and persuaded the Mughal Emperor to grant monopoly trading rights to the East India Company. By the late eighteenth century the East India Company had also emerged as a major political power in India with responsibilities for law, order, administration, trade, defence and diplomacy. By this time the company – run by London merchants – resembled a state more than a private company.

Work

1. Who were the Mughals?
2. Explain how European nations and trading companies exploited wars in India to increase their power.
3. Read **Interpretation D**. Explain in your own words what the author is saying about how powerful the East India Company became.
4. How did Robert Clive and Warren Hastings each contribute to the growth of British control in India?
5. Suggest reasons why the British government took away more control of India from the EIC in the late eighteenth and nineteenth centuries.

▼ **E** *India 1600–1773: how more and more of India gradually came under British control*

Timeline

1600	1612	1638	1658	1668	1707	1757	1763	1773
East India Company is founded	First East India Company trading post is set up in Surat	East India Company trading post is set up in Madras	Aurangzeb becomes the ruling Mughal Emperor	East India Company trading post is set up in Bombay	Aurangzeb dies; Mughal control is weak	Battle of Plassey; East India Company takes control of Bengal	Robert Clive becomes Governor and Commander-in-Chief of the East India Company's army	Government of India Act; Warren Hastings becomes Governor General of India

The Indian Rebellion of 1857

By the 1850s, most of India was ruled by a British company – the East India Company. Many of the British people who worked for the EIC lived in great luxury in India and made huge fortunes. The British ignored or replaced long-standing Indian traditions, rights and customs. They also replaced the aristocracy. This led to widespread frustration and discontentment in the Indian population. To help 'protect' the British in India – and to make sure things ran smoothly – British soldiers were stationed there. The army also recruited local Indians as soldiers, called **Sepoys**. On 10 May 1857, a group of Sepoys shot dead a number of British officers. The Indian rebellion – or the War of Independence – that followed lasted over a year, until June 1858. What caused the fighting, and why does the same event have different names?

Objectives

▶ **Explain** the causes and consequences of the Indian Rebellion.

▶ **Explore** how the events of 1857–58 can be interpreted differently.

Sepoys and rebellion

According to Queen Victoria (reign: 1837–1901), the aim of the British Empire was to 'protect the poor natives and advance civilisation'. It was clear, then, that there was more to the empire than just the financial benefits. British empire-builders felt they were superior to the indigenous people who lived in the colonies, who were a different colour and worshipped in a different way. In India, the British claimed that they were improving the country, by building railways, roads, schools and hospitals, rather than exploiting it.

However, in the army, the Sepoys were very unhappy. They felt that they weren't treated very well, had little hope of promotion and were often the first to be sent to the most dangerous places. Some Sepoys also felt that they were being pressured into converting to Christianity.

This build-up of anger boiled over into rebellion in 1857, when new rifles were delivered to the troops with a new method of loading the bullets. And it was these new bullets, and the cartridges that held them, that led to the start of one of the British Empire's bloodiest rebellions.

The spark

In January 1857, a new Enfield rifle was given to each Indian soldier. The bullet (which fired from the rifle) and the gunpowder that fired it were packaged together in a cartridge. Loading the cartridge was complicated: it involved biting off the top of the cartridge, pouring the gunpowder into the gun and then ramming the rest of the cartridge with the bullet inside down into the gun. The problem for the Hindu and Muslim Sepoys was that the new cartridges were covered in grease to make them slide down easily.

▼ **SOURCE A** *The image from the cover of* Lloyd's Sketches of Indian Life, *published in 1890, showing an Indian soldier waiting on a British woman*

Key Word

Sepoy

Fact

The majority of Sepoys took part in the rebellion – but not all of them. Thousands, including the Gurkhas, the Sikhs and the Pathan regiments, remained loyal to the British. Even today, the Gurkhas who fight in the British army have a long-standing reputation for loyalty to it. The very large Bengali element in the British army in India were thought to be responsible for the rebellion. Subsequently recruitment came from the Punjab, Sikhs and Gurkhas – the groups that the British felt made the best soldiers.

Because the soldiers had to bite off the top of the greasy cartridge, it meant that they got grease in their mouths. It was rumoured that the grease was made from animal fat, probably (but not definitely) a mixture of pork and beef fat. This was the worst possible mixture for Hindus and Muslims – Hindus don't eat beef because cows are sacred to them, and Muslims are forbidden to eat pork.

The Sepoys objected to the new cartridges, but they were largely ignored. When 85 Sepoys refused to use the cartridges in Meerut on 9 May 1857, they were arrested and sent to jail for ten years. The day after, a group of Sepoys broke into revolt in Meerut. They killed British officers, freed the imprisoned Sepoys and set fire to army barracks and the homes of British civilians living in the area. Other Sepoys rioted in support, and soon the whole of northern India was engulfed in rebellion.

▼ **B** *A cross-section diagram showing the new Enfield rifle cartridge*

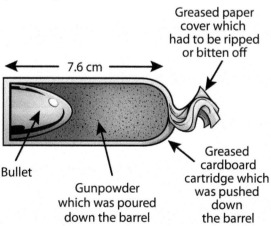

▼ **INTERPRETATION C** *An illustration from* The Heroes of History, *published in the twentieth century. It shows the Siege of Lucknow, when British soldiers were surrounded and attacked by Indian rebels on 1 July 1857. The siege ended in November when support for the British arrived.*

India at war

The main battles were fought in Delhi, Cawnpore and Lucknow. The massacre of 200 British women and children at Cawnpore (July 1857), known as the Bibighar Massacre, outraged the British. Back in Britain, Queen Victoria was horrified and the public cried for blood. Soon, 70,000 fresh troops were sent to India armed with the latest Colt revolvers made in America. Revenge was violent, bloody and swift.

Work

1 a What is a Sepoy?
  b Why were some Sepoys unhappy at this time?
2 a Study diagram **B**, the Enfield rifle cartridge cross-section. Write a short explanation of what a cartridge is.
  b Explain what caused the 1857 rebellion. You need to include what the British did in January 1857 – and why Hindu and Muslim Sepoys objected so strongly.

When some Muslim **mutineers** were captured, they were sewn into pig skins before they were hanged. One British soldier wrote of a giant tree with 130 Sepoys hanging from its branches. An equally horrible punishment was to strap the rebels across the barrel of a gun, which was then fired.

▼ **SOURCE D** *A poem about the reaction to the massacres in India, written by British poet Martin Tupper in 1857 at the time of the rebellion:*

> And England, now avenge their wrongs by vengeance deep and dire,
>
> Cut out their cancer with the sword, and burn it out with fire,
>
> Destroy those traitor regions, hang every pariah hound,
>
> And hunt them down to death, in all hills and cities around.

▼ **SOURCE E** *This cartoon appeared in* Punch *magazine in August 1857 and is called 'The British Lion's Vengeance on the Bengal Tiger'. It shows a British lion (representing Britain) attacking a Bengal tiger (representing India) that had attacked an English woman and child. The cartoon received much attention at the time.*

▼ **INTERPRETATION F** *In an account written in 1884, Vishnubhat Godse describes his experience of the British attack on the fort of Jhansi in April 1858:*

> The English began entering the city and shooting down every man that they saw and setting fire to houses. They first commenced burning and killing in the Halvaipura quarter. They sought out males from the age of five to the age of eighty and killed them... Thousands of white soldiers entered the city from all sides and commenced massacring people. The terror in the city at this time was immeasurable. The screaming and crying was endless.

The end and aftermath

The conflict continued for another year. Peace was finally declared on 8 July 1858, but the rebellion had shocked the British. For a long time it had looked as if the British might be defeated by the Sepoys, and politicians were taken aback by the ferocity of feeling that had been shown in India against the British.

After the events, the British were a lot more careful about how they governed India. They still wanted India as part of the British Empire of course, but the running of the country was taken away from the East India Company and replaced with direct rule by the British government. A new government department (the India Office) was set up, and a **viceroy** was put in charge of India on behalf of Queen Victoria.

Before the rebellion, the British policy in India had been to introduce British ideas about religion and education, which threatened the Hindu, Muslim and Sikh ways of life. After 1858, the British tried to interfere less with religious matters, and started to allow Indians more say in the running of India by allowing them jobs in local government. Although the number of Indians gaining jobs in local government was on a limited scale, a new, professional middle class of Indian citizen emerged: they were able to use English in addition to their own language, and to learn about new technology and methods of organisation that the British were bringing into the country. In time, the Indian Universities

Act created universities in Calcutta, Bombay and Madras. This was to have a major long-term impact on Britain's relationship with India.

▼ **SOURCE G** *Adapted from Queen Victoria's Proclamation to India, November 1858, in which she commented on the new way of running India:*

> We hold ourselves bound by the same obligations of duty which bind us to our other subjects, so it is our will that our subjects of whatever race or creed, be freely and impartially admitted to offices in our service, the duties of which they may be qualified by their education, ability and integrity, duly to discharge.

▼ **INTERPRETATION H** *Adapted from a BBC interview with historian and author William Dalrymple, September 2006:*

> The Indian Freedom Movement was led by [educated Indians] who emerged from English-language schools after 1857, and who by-and-large used modern Western structures and methods – political parties, strikes and protest marches – to gain their freedom. Had 1857 not happened, modern Indian history might have taken a quite different course.

Mutiny, rebellion or war of independence?

Historians often give names to different events (the Peasants' Revolt, the English Civil War and so on) – but there is no universally agreed name for the events of 1857–58. At the time in Britain, it was known as the 'Indian Mutiny' or the 'Sepoy Rebellion'. It is often still called this in Britain today. However, for Indians today, it is most often referred to as the 'War of Independence' or the 'Great Rebellion'. It is looked upon as the first episode in the great struggle against the British for an independent India. Indeed, in 2007 the Indian government celebrated the 150th anniversary of it with special events and ceremonies.

Practice Question

Explain the significance of the Indian Rebellion on the development of the British Empire.   **8 marks**

[Taken from AQA 2016 Paper 2 specimen material]

Key Words

mutineer   viceroy

▼ **INTERPRETATION I** *Adapted from a quote in a section entitled 'The Indian Freedom Struggle', from the official Indian government website, india.gov.in. The website was set up in 2005 (and updated in 2012) to celebrate the Great Rebellion of 1857–58:*

> The Hindus, Muslims and Sikhs and all the other brave sons of India fought shoulder to shoulder to throw out the British.

Work

1   Why do you think the punishments given to the Indian rebels by the British were so brutal?

2   Read **Source D**. Do you think Martin Tupper was a supporter of the Sepoys or a supporter of the British? Give reasons for your answer.

3   Look at **Source E**.
    a   Describe what is happening in the cartoon.
    b   What point do you think the cartoonist was trying to get across?

4   How did the British change the way India was governed as a result of the events of 1857?

5   How useful are **Sources E** and **G** to a historian studying the British reaction to the Indian Rebellion of 1857?

Extension

Read **Interpretation H**. What is the author saying about the long-term impact of the Indian Rebellion? You may wish to read ahead to Chapter 10 about events in twentieth-century India to help you answer this question.

Study Tip

Why do you think the events of 1857 are given different names?

7.3A What was the impact of empire on Britain and India?

India was the largest and richest of all the territories in Britain's empire. In 1858, a viceroy appointed by the British was put directly in charge of the country and ran it on behalf of Queen Victoria. The queen even gave herself an extra title, Empress of India, in addition to her traditional title of Queen of Great Britain and Ireland. Indeed, India was the colony that many people in Britain treasured most – even calling it 'the jewel in the crown'. So what impact did the British make on India? What was British rule like for Indians? And what impact did the British rule of India have on Britain itself?

Objectives

▶ **Examine** the different factors that affected the British Empire in India in the nineteenth and early twentieth centuries.

▶ **Assess** ways in which the British takeover of India could be viewed both positively and negatively.

There is little doubt that the British made a huge impact on India. However, there is much debate over whether the British had a positive or a negative overall influence. Some argue that any foreign interference in another country is a bad thing, while others would say that it is a good thing if a nation's rule of another country brings improvements. Below are some insights into British rule in India that will help you assess the impact that Britain had.

India's economic resources

British businessmen, merchants and traders saw India as an opportunity to make lots of money. They used India to build up personal fortunes, making some of them the richest people in the world. They would buy (or take) raw materials from India (such as tea, coffee, sugar cane, gemstones, gold, silver, silk and spices) and sell them for a high price in Britain. In the mid-1800s, the tea trade alone was worth £30 million a year! Trading in goods not only made money for the traders, but created jobs for both Indians and the British in shipping, transportation and sales. However, the British improved things too: they introduced an irrigation programme in the countryside, which increased the amount of land available for farming by eight times. Also, they developed coal mining, something that had not existed before. It is important to consider that these innovations and developments were paid for by British investors, whose priority was to make a profit for themselves rather than improve the life of Indian people.

▼ **SOURCE A** *This engraving was published in a London news magazine in 1853, depicting a shipment of Indian gold being unloaded in the East India Docks, London. Note the police guarding the area.*

Building factories

Many areas in India became industrialised in the same way that British towns and cities were in the 1800s. Factories were built there, producing goods such as cotton and woollen cloth, and flour. Local Indians worked in these factories and mills, which were owned by British businessmen. India was also a place where British-made factory goods could be sold too. It was common for Indian-grown cotton to be shipped back to Britain, made into something (such as a shirt or trousers) in a British factory – and then taken back to India to be sold there.

Communications: railways and transport

The British built over 30,000 kilometres of railways and 130,000 bridges all over India. This was important for the economic development of India, as goods and people could travel quickly over vast areas and distant parts of the country could be linked together. The total British investment in India amounted to more than an estimated £400 million by 1914. This included not only railways, but also canals, roads, factories, mines and farms. Some argue that this was done simply to exploit the country and make huge profits, which were taken back to Britain. Others say that the investment created an important legacy that still survives today.

▼ **SOURCE B** *This railway station was built in Bombay (now Mumbai) in 1897. It was known as Victoria Station until 1996, when it was renamed after a seventeenth-century Hindu king. Today, Indian Railways is one of the world's largest employers, with an amazing 1.6 million employees.*

Improved health?

The British made an impact on health in India too. They introduced a vaccine and treatment programme to fight killer diseases such as malaria and smallpox, and improved sewage systems and water supplies. As a result of these changes, life expectancy increased. However, there were devastating famines that struck India in the late 1800s. Millions died of starvation. Many blamed the British for helping to cause the famines because they had forced Indian farmers to replace food crops such as rice and wheat with high value crops that the British could sell in Britain, such as cotton, tea and oil seeds.

Culture and society: the law and education

The British created a legal system based on the one in Britain. They felt that their legal system was the most advanced in the world and should be used as a model for other nations where possible. High courts were set up in Madras, Calcutta and Bombay and parts of Indian law were built into the new legal code. Hindu and Muslim judges made sure that the British did not forget about Indian traditions and customs when dealing with legal matters. The British also had a major impact on education, opening thousands of schools and colleges. This increased English language learning, which benefited British traders and meant that Indians had greater access to new knowledge in science humanities, and literature. This British-style education also meant that many Indians adopted the same modern, democratic, liberal views as Western countries.

Work

1   Write a sentence or two explaining the following terms: viceroy; Empress of India; 'the jewel in the crown'.

2   Make two lists: one of the positive things that British rule brought to India, and one of the negative things about British rule.

What was the impact of empire on Britain and India?

The impact of the British Raj on Britain

Arguably the most notable impact of British rule in India was the boost it gave to British industry and wealth. India provided a steady supply of raw materials into Britain, which were converted into finished products in British factories and then sold back to countries in the British Empire, including India itself. This created jobs for British businessmen and merchants, sailors, dockworkers, factory workers, shopkeepers and so on. By the late 1800s, for example, it has been estimated that around a quarter of Britain's total exports went to India – and by the early 1900s these exports were worth nearly £140 million!

Fact

The term 'British Raj' was used to describe the period of British rule in India between 1858 and 1947. The word 'raj' is Hindi for 'rule'. The British Raj had its own flag.

British rule in India brought other benefits to Britain, most notably the Indian army. This army was used in all parts of the British Empire, and fought bravely and decisively in both the First and Second World Wars. It is notable that in the First World War, by December 1914, one in every three soldiers fighting for Britain in France was from India.

▼ **SOURCE C** *The British viceroy of India, Lord Curzon, wrote the following to the Conservative MP (and future Prime Minister) Lord Balfour, indicating that the Indian army was viewed as vital to Britain's power on the world stage:*

As long as we rule India, we are the greatest power in the world. If we lose it we shall straightaway drop to a third rate power.

There were also some more subtle impacts in Britain. Indian tea became a popular drink and Indian food became more and more common in people's homes. Queen Victoria employed an Indian secretary to teach her Hindi and Urdu, and had Indian dishes on most of her dinner menus. Indian words, such as 'bangle', 'shampoo', 'pyjamas' and 'cash', became commonly used, and many grand buildings (like the Royal Pavilion in Brighton) were built in an Indian style.

▼ **INTERPRETATION D** *Adapted from* Pax Britannica, *written by modern historian James Morris in 1968. At the time he wrote, Ceylon (now Sri Lanka) was classified as part of India and was under British rule:*

Ceylon was unified under British rule in 1815. Over the next 80 years, the British built 3700 kilometres of road and 4600 kilometres of railway. They raised the area of land used for farming from 160,000 hectares to 1.3 million hectares, the livestock from 230,000 to 1.5 million, the post offices from 4 to 250, the telegraph lines from 0 to 2500 kilometres, the schools from 170 to 2900, the hospitals from 0 to 65, the annual amount of goods shipped abroad from 68,000 tonnes to 6.3 million tonnes.

Divided opinions

The issue of British control and influence in India has always been controversial and has often been interpreted differently. Some argue that India benefited from British influence in some ways. By 1900, the British had built nearly 80,000 kilometres of road, as well as railways, schools and hospitals. They built dams and dug nearly 12,000 kilometres of canal. They also introduced a new legal system and helped settle ancient feuds between rival areas and regions – whether the Indians wanted these things or not. It cannot be denied that the British invested a lot of money into India, but they made an enormous amount of money too.

Furthermore, India suffered greatly in many ways. British customs were forced onto people, and local traditions, cultures and religions tended to be ignored. Indian workers were often exploited, the country's raw materials were taken back to Britain, and native lands were seized. If there was ever any resistance, the British army usually came down very hard on the rebels.

▼ SOURCE E *Adapted from the Independence Day Resolution (1930), a public statement that declared the Indian National Congress and Indian nationalists would work for complete self-rule, independent of the British Empire*

> […] it is the inalienable right of the Indian people […] to have freedom and to enjoy the fruits of their toil […] so that they may have full opportunities of growth […] The British Government in India has not only deprived the Indian people of their freedom but has based itself on the exploitation of the masses, and has ruined India economically, politically, culturally, and spiritually.

▼ SOURCE F *An illustration from a French newspaper about the Indian famine of the late 1800s; approximately six million Indians died – and many Indians blamed the British for not doing enough*

▼ SOURCE G *Florence Nightingale, the famous British nurse and reformer, said in the late 1800s about the Indian famine:*

> We do not care enough to stop them dying slow and terrible deaths from things we could easily stop. We have taken their land, and we rule it, for our good, not theirs.

▼ SOURCE H *Adapted from* Indian Home Rule, *written by Mohandas K. Gandhi in 1938:*

> India has become impoverished by their [Britain's] government. They take away our money from year to year. The most important jobs are reserved for themselves. We are kept in a state of slavery. They behave insolently towards us and disregard our feelings.

Work

1 Create a poster called 'The British in India'. Using no more than ten words show both the positives and the negatives of British rule there.

2 Suggest reasons why the British rule of India divides opinions, even today.

3 a What point does **Source E** make about British rule in India? What about **Source H**?

   b How useful is **Source F** to a historian studying British rule in India?

Extension

The English language has absorbed many Indian words, such as 'bangle', 'cash' and 'shampoo'. Research other Indian words that are commonly used in English today. What about other countries within the British Empire? What words are used from Africa, Australia or indigenous America?

Practice Question

Have the economic benefits been the main consequence of British rule in India?   **16 marks**
SPaG: 4 marks

Study Tip

Consider the social and cultural consequences of British rule as well in your answer (see pages 54–57).

The scramble for Africa

— Political
— Religions
— Economic

Until the 1800s, European countries weren't really interested in Africa – unless it was to capture and enslave people from the west of Africa. Between 1562 and 1807 (when Britain stopped slave trading), British ships took around three million Africans into slavery in America and the Caribbean. But even as late as 1870, only ten per cent of Africa was controlled by European countries. Yet by 1900, European nations controlled over 90 per cent of Africa – and Britain was one of the nations that took the most land: 16 colonies were added to the British Empire between 1870 and 1900. Why did this happen?

Objectives

▶ **Define** the 'scramble for Africa'.

▶ **Explain** why Britain joined in the scramble for Africa in the late 1800s.

▶ **Examine** trade and missionary activity in Africa in the nineteenth century.

Why were European countries interested in Africa?

By the 1860s, France, Germany and the USA had all become powerful nations. They each had huge armies and navies, and their factories produced goods that were sold all over the world. Until then, Britain had been the world's leading power in both industry and trade, but now there were some serious rivals.

Explorers and missionaries (such as Britain's David Livingstone) brought back tales of African gold, diamonds and ivory – as well as 'cash crops' such as rubber, coffee and timber – so some of the world's richest countries saw Africa as an opportunity to get even richer. They thought that if they could take over huge areas of Africa, they could sell their goods to the people who lived there, and take valuable raw materials from the land. After 1870, treatments were available to combat diseases that were common in Africa (such as malaria), so European exploration increased. Some of Europe's major nations went 'empire-building' in order to become richer than their neighbouring countries. Between 1880 and 1900, they raced to grab as much of Africa for themselves as they could. This became known as the 'scramble for Africa'.

Christian missionaries also felt it was their duty to convert Africans to Christianity. They travelled through Africa preaching the benefits of Christianity, as well as setting up schools and hospitals. Europeans often referred to Africa as the 'dark continent', and missionaries felt it was their role to 'enlighten' it.

The scramble begins

In the late 1870s, several European nations started to 'claim' land in Africa. The French and Belgians began to colonise much of the west of Africa, while the Germans and the British were interested in the east and the south. Portugal, Italy and Spain joined in the land grab. To prevent a war erupting between the European powers, their leaders held a conference in Berlin, Germany during the winter of 1884–85, to decide which nation could take which areas. Little attempt was made to understand the wishes or needs of the Africans themselves, so differences in race, language, culture and traditions were ignored as the European nations grabbed what they could.

▼ **SOURCE A** *British politician Lord Rosebery, who became Prime Minister in 1894, made a speech in 1893, during the 'scramble for Africa'. He stated:*

> It is said that our empire is already big enough and doesn't need extension. That would be true if the world were elastic, but it is not. At present we are 'pegging out claims for the future'. We have to remember that it is part of our heritage to make sure that the world is shaped by us. It must be English-speaking. We have to look forward to the future of our race. We will fail in our duty if we fail to take our share of the world.

▼ **SOURCE B** *A well-known African saying; its origins are unclear but it has been said by both Jomo Kenyatta, independent Kenya's first Prime Minister (1963–64) and first President (1964–78), and Archbishop Desmond Tutu, a South African social rights activist and bishop:*

> When the missionaries arrived, the Africans had the land and the missionaries had the Bible. They taught us how to pray with our eyes closed. When we opened them, they had the land and we had the Bible.

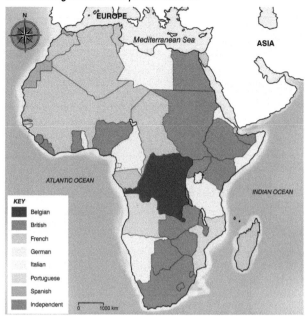

▼ **C** *Africa in 1900, after the 'scramble', showing the areas controlled by various European countries*

KEY
- Belgian
- British
- French
- German
- Italian
- Portuguese
- Spanish
- Independent

0   1000 km

The British scramble

Britain took over 16 huge areas of land (or colonies) in Africa during the 'scramble', including Sudan, Nigeria, Kenya, Egypt and Northern and Southern Rhodesia (now Zimbabwe and Zambia). In fact, Britain's land ran in an almost unbroken line from Egypt in the north of Africa to South Africa in the south. In total, the British had claimed 32 per cent of Africa by 1900. Britain's control of key areas of African land (in southern Africa, for example) was important because it lay along part of Britain's sea route to India.

African resistance

African people fought fiercely at times to defend their lands, but the invention of the Maxim gun (a type of machine gun) gave the European armies a great advantage over the Africans, who were mainly armed with spears and swords. Sometimes, Africans won major victories over European countries (such as in the Anglo-Zulu War of 1879), but more often than not the European invaders wiped out the African forces. After they were defeated, many Africans suffered hardship

▼ **SOURCE D** *Although they were later defeated at Rorke's Drift, Zulu forces won a resounding victory over the British at Isandlwana during the Anglo-Zulu War. Here, Cetshwayo, the Zulu king, rallies his warriors:*

> I am sending you out against the whites, who have invaded Zululand and driven away our cattle. You are to go against the column at Rorke's Drift and drive it back into Natal... You will attack by daylight...

and hunger as their traditional way of life was destroyed. Some were forced to work as cheap labour in mines or on huge British-owned farms growing tea, coffee, cotton or cocoa for export back to Britain.

▼ **SOURCE E** *A French cartoon from 1884 about the Berlin Conference of 1884–85, at which European leaders met to agree claims to African territory. Otto von Bismarck (Chancellor of Germany) is shown holding a knife over a sliced-up cake representing Africa. His fellow delegates at the table look shocked.*

Work

1. In your own words, explain what is meant by the term 'scramble for Africa'.

2. Why do you think Britain was so keen to take part in the 'scramble'?

3. Explain how each of the following contributed to the 'scramble for Africa': political factors (rivalry between nations); economic factors (trade); religious factors (Christianity); explorers; technology; medical progress.

4. Look at **Source A**. According to this source, what are the reasons for Britain's expansion into Africa?

Practice Question

How useful is **Source E** to a historian studying attitudes to European expansion in Africa? **8 marks**

Study Tip

Make sure you link what you know with what you can see in the picture.

Why is Cecil Rhodes such a controversial figure?

Cecil Rhodes is one of Britain's most well-known empire-builders. Streets, schools, and even two African countries – Southern and Northern Rhodesia (now Zimbabwe and Zambia) – were named after him. When he died, statues of him were erected all over the world. However, in 2015, a Cecil Rhodes statue was removed from the University of Cape Town in South Africa. Why have opinions of Rhodes changed over the years?

Objectives

▶ **Define** 'social Darwinism'.

▶ **Examine** the role played by Cecil Rhodes in the 'scramble for Africa'.

▶ **Assess** why Cecil Rhodes has attracted both admiration and hatred.

◀ **SOURCE A** *The removal of the Cecil Rhodes statue, in April 2015, from the University of Cape Town*

What did Rhodes think about the British Empire?

Rhodes was an **imperialist**, and believed that Britain should extend its power and influence over other parts of the world by any means possible. He believed he could take Darwin's theory of evolution, which said that weaker animals would die out and stronger ones would evolve and survive, and apply it to countries or peoples. Darwin's theory made Rhodes think it was right for the stronger (and therefore 'superior') Britain to take over weaker countries. This belief – called **social Darwinism** – was frequently used to justify European imperialism in Africa and other areas of the world.

Key Biography

Cecil Rhodes (1853–1902)

- Born in Bishop's Stortford.
- In 1870, went to Cape Colony, the southern part of Africa controlled by the British, to work in gold and diamond mines. Soon made a fortune.
- In 1881, was elected to the Cape Colony parliament, and in 1890 became its Prime Minister.
- In 1888, formed a company, De Beers, which owned most of the gold and diamond fields in southern Africa. He then used his money and political skills to gain control of more land. When gold and diamonds were discovered in the Transvaal, an area controlled by Dutch settlers known as **Boers**, Rhodes was refused permission to mine there. He tried to get rid of the Boer leader, Paul Kruger, by force, but failed, and Britain was dragged into wars with the Boers. The British eventually won and gained more territory, but Rhodes died in 1902, a few months before the wars ended.

▼ **SOURCE B** *Adapted from an essay written by Cecil Rhodes in* Confessions of Faith, *1877. When Rhodes writes 'Anglo-Saxon' he means 'white British', and he thought of the British as a 'master race', many years before the term became associated with Adolf Hitler and the Nazis:*

> I contend that we are the finest race in the world and that the more of the world we inhabit the better it is for the human race. What an alteration there would be if Africans were brought under Anglo-Saxon influence.

Assessing Cecil Rhodes

Rhodes was a controversial figure when he was alive, as well as today. He attracted criticism when his actions in the Transvaal led to the wars in which thousands died. While a politician, he introduced an act that pushed black people from their lands and increased taxes on their homes. He also made it harder for black people to vote.

Undoubtedly, though, Rhodes had many supporters, who argued that he brought vast wealth to Britain and made the southern part of Africa into a more stable and developed place. When he died, he left money in a scholarship fund that allowed overseas students to study at Oxford University, and many institutions, including the University of Cape Town, benefited from his generosity.

Some would argue that Rhodes was a man 'of his time' and that we shouldn't judge his actions and beliefs by today's standards. Ideas like social Darwinism were widely accepted at the time, and Rhodes was simply doing what lots of people and countries were doing. However, others argue that there should be no excuse for a person's actions and beliefs, no matter when they lived. We look at Rhodes differently today because we have contrasting views about empire and race to those that were common in previous centuries.

▼ **SOURCE C** *This cartoon appeared in* Punch *magazine in 1892, next to an article about Rhodes' plan to extend an electrical telegraph line from Cape Town in the south to Egypt's capital city Cairo in the north. Both Cape Colony and Egypt were under British control.*

Key Words

imperialist   social Darwinism   Boer

▼ **INTERPRETATION D** *Adapted from an article called 'Cecil Rhodes' colonial legacy must fall – not his statue', which appeared in* The Guardian *in March 2015, written by Siya Mnyanda, a politics and philosophy graduate from the University of Cape Town (UCT):*

> Dr Max Price, vice chancellor of UCT, summed up the contradictions by saying that although Rhodes was considered a 'great man', the attitudes and means he used 'were not right'. [Price said] 'He was racist. He used power and money to oppress others. So on balance he was a villain.' [...]
>
> But as a black UCT alumnus [former student], who walked past that statue for four years, I think Rhodes should be left exactly where he is. Removing him omits an essential part of the university's history that has contributed to everything good, bad and ugly about it – and arguably the country too.

Extension

Read **Interpretation D**. Describe the two views of Rhodes that Dr Max Price describes. Why does the writer of the article think the statue of Rhodes should stay? Why do you think there are different views of Cecil Rhodes?

Practice Question

Explain the significance of Cecil Rhodes for the development of the British Empire in Africa.

8 marks

Study Tip

Remember the definition of 'significance' here. A significant person was not only important at the time, and affected many people's lives deeply, for a long time, but they are also still relevant in today's world.

Work

1   Make a list of things that Rhodes either said or did that shows him to be: an imperialist; a social Darwinist.

2   Do you think the students of the University of Cape Town were right to vote for the removal of the statue? Discuss with a partner, and give reasons for your answer.

3   How useful is **Source C** to a historian studying the aims of Britain in Africa?

8.3 | Why did Britain get involved in Egypt?

Look at map **A** and **Source B**. They show the Suez Canal in Egypt, an important trade link between the Mediterranean Sea and the Indian Ocean. The 164-kilometre-long canal is in northern Africa. Its opening in 1869 meant that countries that wished to trade with India (and other eastern countries) did not have to sail their ships all around the vast continent of Africa. This was safer and faster, so goods could travel much quicker. Britain took no part in the building of the canal, and yet by 1882 it had managed to gain control of both Egypt and the Suez Canal. How did Britain gain control of this important canal? How and why did Britain get involved in this area of Africa?

The Suez Canal: a new route

▼ **A** *A map of the Suez Canal, and the different shipping distances from London to Mumbai. The canal reduces the journey distance by over 4000 nautical miles, making the journey around two weeks shorter.*

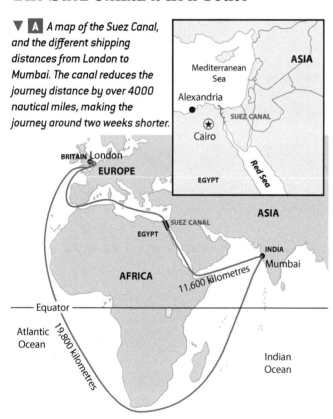

▼ **SOURCE B** *A hand-coloured postcard showing Ferdinand de Lesseps opening the Suez Canal in November 1869. It was funded and built jointly by France and Egypt. Initially Britain saw the building of the canal as a threat to its global maritime empire.*

The British government took no part in paying for the Suez Canal, or its construction. However, the route was vital for Britain's trade with India as it meant that ships could take a short cut. Within a few years of the canal opening, around 80 per cent of the ships using the canal were British. Furthermore, in the event of another rebellion in India, or problems in other British colonies in the area, the time saved by using the canal could be vital. So to secure the route, the British government bought a controlling share in the canal from the Egyptians when they got into financial difficulty. The deal to buy this share of the canal was organised by British Prime Minister Benjamin Disraeli, who arranged for the government to borrow £4 million from a famous banker and politician, Lionel de Rothschild. When Disraeli heard the news that the sale had gone through he said to Queen Victoria, 'It is settled; you have it, madam. Four million pounds!' Lord Curzon, who was Viceroy of India between 1899 and 1905, described the canal as 'the determining influence of every considerable movement of British power to the east and south of the Mediterranean'.

Egypt in trouble

Just a few years after receiving money from the sale of their shares in the canal, the Egyptian government was again in economic difficulties. The British, in partnership with the French, gave money to the Egyptians in return for control over much of their trade, railways, post offices and ports. But in 1882, the Egyptians rebelled against what they saw as interference from the British and French. In one riot in Alexandria, a number of British people were killed, and the British responded by ordering the navy to bomb the city. The French, however, refused to get involved.

Occupying Egypt

The bombing of Alexandria in July 1882 caused heavy damage to the city, destroying its defences. A few days later, 24,000 soldiers from Britain and 7000 soldiers from British India entered Egypt. They began taking control of major towns and cities, including the capital, Cairo. Over 40 navy warships secured the Suez Canal.

So, by 1882, Britain had gained control of another African country. Thousands of soldiers were permanently based in Egypt and British navy warships defended the Suez Canal. Control of Egypt also gave Britain responsibility for Sudan – a country that the Egyptians controlled. In 1884, a religious leader known as the Madhi led an uprising in Sudan against the British and Egyptians. The rebels killed the British commander, General Charles Gordon, and held out for many years. However, between 1886 and 1888 the British, under Lord Kitchener, led a series of brutal military campaigns against supporters of the Madhi. Eventually, in 1899 Sudan, like Egypt before, came under British control.

Work

1   What is the Suez Canal?

2   Why do you think the Suez Canal was constructed?

3   Why do you think the British were particularly interested in the Suez Canal?

4   In your own words, explain how Britain gained control of both Egypt and Sudan.

5   Conduct research to write a news article titled 'The Suez Canal: then and now' to report on what has happened to the Suez Canal since the 1800s. Is it still under British control? If not, how did the British lose control? How important is the Suez Canal today?

▼ **SOURCE C** *A Punch cartoon from 1876 called 'The Lion's Share'. It is commenting on the sale of shares in the Suez Canal.*

The Boer War of 1899–1902

In the 1800s, two groups of Europeans competed for control of land in southern Africa – the British and the Boers. The Boers were descendants of Dutch settlers who had gone to southern Africa in the 1650s. They were mostly farmers (*boer* is the Dutch word for farmer) and their colony was named Cape Colony. In 1806, the British invaded Cape Colony and it soon officially became part of the British Empire. The Boers resented British control and left Cape Colony to head north. They set up two new colonies named the Transvaal and the Orange Free State.

Objectives

▶ **Identify** why the British fought wars against the Boers in South Africa.

▶ **Assess** the consequences of the wars, in particular the Boer War of 1899–1902.

▼ **A** *This map shows the two Boer colonies – the Transvaal and the Orange Free State. Their flags are based on the red, white and blue of the Dutch flag. The map also shows the British-controlled lands of Cape Colony and Natal.*

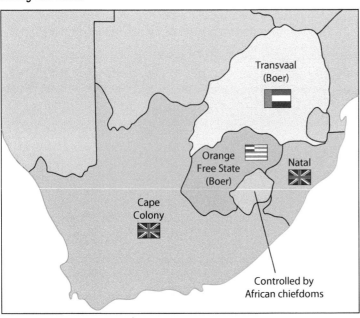

In 1886, gold was discovered in the Boer states. British businessman Cecil Rhodes (who lived in Cape Colony) saw this as an opportunity and opened dozens of mines inside Boer territory. Thousands of British workers arrived in the area and soon the Boers felt their land was under threat. The Boer leader, Paul Kruger, refused to give the British workers any political rights. Tensions reached breaking point when Cecil Rhodes sponsored a plan to overthrow Kruger and replace him with a British ruler. Rhodes' plan failed – and relations between the British and the Boers got worse. The British began to send more troops to Cape Colony, and placed them along the borders with the Boer states. In 1899, another war broke out.

The Second Boer War, 1899–1902

Early on in this war, known as the Second Boer War, the small Boer army stunned the British with a series of victories. The British had completely underestimated the Boers, who were highly skilled fighters, armed with modern guns, who knew the terrain well.

First Boer War breaks out: 1867–81

In 1867, diamonds were discovered in the new Boer states. The British government tried to get the Boers to unite their states with the British ones (Cape Colony and Natal), but the Boers refused. British troops were sent in to try to force the Boers to accept British rule, but the Boers fought back brilliantly. At the Battle of Majuba Hill in February 1881, the British suffered a heavy defeat and put their takeover plans on hold.

▼ **B** *Boer soldiers adopted brilliant military tactics against the British forces*

No military uniform, so they easily blended in with local settlers

Armed with the latest German-made military rifles and artillery

All fighters were mobile, on horseback; unlike the British, there were no **infantry** soldiers to slow down the unit

Fact

Some black farm workers helped the Boer fighters, moving ammunition, weapons and supplies. Others worked for the British, for example as scouts or drivers, or fighting in the army.

Fighters often 'lived off the land' by foraging for food or capturing enemy supplies; the British needed long supply chains to keep their vast groups of soldiers fed and armed

Mainly fought in small groups (5–12 fighters), so units were hard to detect and moved around easily, capturing supplies and attacking troops and communication lines when least expected; these tactics were known as **guerrilla** (Spanish for 'little war') tactics

▼ **SOURCE C** *Three generations of Boer War soldiers in 1890; (from left to right) P. J. Lemmer (age 65), J. D. L. Botha (age 15) and G. J. Pretorius (age 43)*

Work

1 a Who were the Boers?
  b Why did the Boers leave Cape Colony?

2 Why do you think the British became interested in the new Boer colonies?

3 Why did war break out in southern Africa in 1899?

4 Look at diagram **B**. Use it to help you explain why the Boer fighters were so successful against the British forces in the early stages of the war.

The Boer War of 1899–1902

The British fight back

In January 1900, the British responded to their losses by sending half a million troops to fight approximately 50,000 Boer soldiers. The British army used all the hi-tech weaponry they had — machine guns, modern rifles and high explosive shells. Yet the Boers refused to surrender and carried out dozens of small raids on British camps, railways and mines. The British responded savagely.

The British commander during the Second Boer War, General Kitchener, decided that the only way to get the Boers to surrender was to introduce a **scorched earth** policy. This meant that British soldiers were instructed to burn down Boer farms, kill the animals, destroy crops and poison drinking

▼ SOURCE D *An Illustration from French newspaper* Le Petit Parisien *from January 1901, showing Boer prisoners in a British camp in the Transvaal. The British soldiers are outside in the white helmets.*

wells. Then Boer men, women and children were rounded up into concentration camps. Out of 116,000 Boers put in these camps, 28,000 (mainly children) died, largely due to disease and illness brought on by poor conditions. There were black concentration camps too; about 130,000 black civilians were rounded up, most of them labourers on Boer farms — and it is thought that at least 20,000 died.

Peace at last

By 1902, both sides were exhausted after years of brutal fighting. Eventually the Boers were forced to surrender, and peace talks began. It was agreed that the Boer states would become British colonies, but the Boers were promised that they could make many of the key decisions in running their lands. In 1910, the Boer states joined with Cape Colony and Natal to form the Union of South Africa, part of the British Empire. However, this Union (commonly known as South Africa) was classed as a **dominion**, rather than a colony, and ran its own affairs.

Consequences of the Boer War of 1899–1902

The Boer War was Britain's biggest twentieth-century 'empire war'. At first in Britain, there was great support for the war and thousands of men volunteered to fight, but enthusiasm for the war was short lived. Around 450,000 British soldiers fought in the war, and nearly 6000 died in battle. A further 16,000 died from illness and wounds sustained in battles. The Boers lost around 7000 of their

90,000 soldiers, and over 28,000 civilians. The war showed how determined the British were to hold onto their empire – at whatever cost.

The Boer War also had an unexpected consequence. Young British men had volunteered to fight in their thousands, but over a third of them were classed as 'unfit for duty'. This worried the government. Unless something was done, how was Britain going to fight its wars in the future?

Around the same time, several special investigations into the lives of the poor started to make headlines. One report found that around 30 per cent of Londoners were so poor that they didn't have enough money to eat properly, despite having full-time jobs!

Finally, in 1906, the government decided to act. One of the first moves was to introduce free school meals for the poorest children. Other measures over the next five years included free medical checks and health treatments in schools. The government also encouraged the teaching of 'domestic science' in schools, which was the study of nutrition, food, clothing, child development, family relationships and household skills. This was a direct result of the fact that so many young people who volunteered to fight in the Boer War were so physically unfit for military service.

After helping children, the government moved on to other sections of society. They introduced unemployment benefit (the 'dole'), sickness pay and old age pensions. They even built Britain's first job centres. Indeed, it seems that a distant war in southern Africa led to many of the ideas that still help the most vulnerable people in our society today.

Extension

One of the most famous battles of the Boer War was fought at a place called Spion Kop in January 1900. Many football clubs named stands in their football grounds after this battle. Find out which clubs have used the word 'kop' when naming one of their stands. Why do you think football clubs would choose to name parts of their ground after this battle?

Fact

The wars in southern Africa in the nineteenth century have many names. For the British they were the Boer Wars – but for the Boers they were the Wars of Independence. Today, most South Africans refer to them as the Anglo-Boer Wars.

Work

1 Explain the following terms:
   a scorched earth policy
   b concentration camp
   c Union of South Africa.

2 Look at **Source D**.
   a In your own words, describe what you can see in the image.
   b At the time this illustration appeared, the French were Britain's rivals in trying to conquer areas of Africa. Do you think this might have had an impact on the way this image was drawn?

3 In your own words, assess the impact of the Boer Wars on British society. Consider the social and political results of the wars in Britain and South Africa.

Practice Question

Were ideas such as imperialism and social Darwinism the main factor driving British involvement in Africa in the nineteenth century?

16 marks
SPaG: 4 marks

Study Tip

Try to write a paragraph about at least one other factor, such as trade or wealth, in your answer.

Celebrating the British Empire

In 1887, Queen Victoria celebrated 50 years as queen. The event was marked by special celebrations, and the public enthusiasm for the queen and her Golden Jubilee resulted in the production of a huge range of souvenirs. These souvenirs form part of what we can call **imperial propaganda**. But what is 'imperial propaganda', and how did it help to spread ideas about Britain and its empire?

Objectives

▶ **Define** 'imperial propaganda'.

▶ **Examine** the variety of methods used to promote the British Empire.

Queen and empire

The British Empire expanded rapidly during the reign of Queen Victoria (reign: 1837–1901). The British government, and the queen herself, knew that a large empire brought trading benefits to Britain and made the country richer. There was also the belief the British had a 'right' to the land and were helping people in conquered nations by teaching them a new, Christian way of life. There was an incorrect belief at the time that Christianity and white skin were 'superior' to other religions and skin colours. Even Queen Victoria said that one of the aims of the British Empire was to 'protect the poor natives and to advance civilisation'. This was a time when most people were very loyal to their queen and their country, and patriotic pride was encouraged – the government realised that if people's enthusiasm for the empire remained high, then it would have their full support when taking over more land abroad.

Books and newspapers helped to fuel people's enthusiasm for the empire. Magazines for young people had such titles as *Union Jack* and *Young England*, and the popular magazine for teenagers, *Boy's Own Paper*, was filled with stories of brave soldiers 'doing their duty' while fighting enemies on behalf of the queen. Newspapers wrote vivid accounts of successful battles overseas, and the spread of the telegraph communication system meant that stories could appear within a day of the event. This certainly made an impact on people: for example, during the Boer War, huge crowds gathered at fairgrounds and music halls to see film clips from the battle front on the newly invented cinema screen. The popularity of the empire at this time meant that companies such as Pears were keen to associate their goods with it as a way of making more money.

▼ **SOURCE A** *A Pears' Soap advert from 1880. Soap was first used widely in the Victorian period. At the time, the advert was thought to show how advanced, clean, civilised and racially superior the British were. This advert links the idea of 'cleanliness', 'whiteness' and 'superiority' together. The white child is shown 'helping' the black child by making him cleaner – and whiter. It plays on the racist idea that 'white is better'.*

Imperial propaganda

The commemorative plate shown in **Source B** does not just commemorate Queen Victoria's Golden Jubilee, it also celebrates the size and power of Britain's empire. A map is included on the plate, highlighting (in red) the areas of the world controlled by the British. Four of those areas are specifically mentioned: Australia, Canada, Cape Colony in southern Africa and India. The plate also shows the amount of goods sold abroad (exports) and goods brought into Britain (imports). The total population of the British Empire is also written. In fact, at this time, pride in the British Empire was at its height, and companies took advantage of that pride to make money.

All sorts of products, from bars of soap to tins of chocolates, were covered with images relating to the glory of the empire. Posters, school books, exhibitions and

parades all conveyed the empire's positive aspects. This was a type of imperial propaganda, in which the positive aspects, ideas and information about the empire were spread in order to influence public opinion and beliefs.

In schools, textbooks were filled with stories of Britain's 'great' empire-builders, such as Cecil Rhodes, and students were taught that a huge empire was Britain's destiny. Poems and music hall songs celebrated the power of Britain and its armed forces, and even nursery rhyme books sometimes had an empire theme. Furthermore, two new societies were formed (the British Empire League and the British Colonial Society) to support the idea of imperialism and to promote loyalty to the British Empire. Although the impact that organisations like these, and imperial propaganda in general, had on the ordinary British citizen is unclear, there is little doubt that they could not escape the promotion of patriotic pride at this time.

▼ **SOURCE C** *A well-known poem from the 1870s; it introduced a new word to the English language – **jingoism** – to define an aggressive attitude towards foreign nations. In the song, the word 'jingo' was used instead of 'Jesus', which was viewed as an inappropriate word to use in a song at the time:*

> We don't want to fight,
> But by jingo if we do,
> We've got the ships,
> We've got the men,
> We've got the money too!

Key Words

imperial propaganda   jingoism

▼ **SOURCE D** *From an 1899 nursey rhyme book called* ABC for Baby Patriots. *It makes reference to the belief that the British thought they were justified in taking over other nations:*

> C is for colonies, rightly we boast,
> That of all the great nations
> Great Britain has most.
> [...]
> F is the flag; which wherever you see,
> You know that beneath it; you're happy and free.

Work

1. Look at **Source A**.
   a. Describe what is happening in the two images in the advert.
   b. Why were British companies so keen to associate themselves with the empire?
   c. Suggest reasons why the advert has been designed in this way.

2. Look at **Source B**.
   a. In your own words, describe the plate.
   b. Suggest two reasons why someone might buy one of these plates.

3. a. Explain what is meant by the term 'imperial propaganda'.
   b. Make a list of methods used to spread positive ideas and messages about the British Empire.
   c. Why do you think the British government was so keen to spread these positive ideas and messages about the British Empire?

Practice Question

How useful is **Source A** to a historian studying attitudes to the British Empire in the late nineteenth century?   **8 marks**

Study Tip

Consider how the source relates to the motives for gaining an empire. What does it suggest about different races? Why would Pears use these ideas in their advertisements?

Irish migration to Britain

People, or groups of people, have always moved between different countries. Some move because they want to (known as **voluntary migration**), while others move because they have no choice and are forced to (called **forced migration**). One of the largest groups to come to Britain in the last few hundred years has been the Irish. There were a number of reasons why they came – and their impact was important. Why did the Irish move? How did people react to their arrival, and what impact did they have?

Objectives

▶ **Examine** reasons why many Irish migrants came to Britain.

▶ **Analyse** the experiences of Irish immigrants.

▶ **Assess** the impact of Irish migration.

Why did the Irish migrate?

There was a huge increase in Irish migration from the late eighteenth century onwards, mainly through the ports of Liverpool and Glasgow. Thousands stayed in those cities, and there are still large Irish communities there now. Most came to escape the extreme poverty in parts of Ireland, and to find better paid work. Many found jobs around the country as **navvies**, building the many new canals, roads and later railways: one third of the navvies who worked on the railways were Irish. They also worked in mines and in cotton mills, in Britain's quickly expanding towns and cities.

There was a great surge in Irish immigration after 1846, when a disease called 'potato blight' ruined the Irish potato harvest. Potatoes formed a major part of the Irish diet at this time, so many people starved. Around one million people (or one eighth of the population) died during famine, either from starvation or from illnesses that their weakened bodies couldn't fight. Hundreds of thousands fled to Britain, peaking in the 1840s and 1850s, when over one and a half million Irish people left their homeland.

Fact

Britain was not the only destination for the Irish – nearly a million travelled to the USA. Today, large communities with Irish ancestry can be found in many US cities including Philadelphia, Chicago and Boston. Many places across the country have annual St Patrick's Day parades; the one in New York is one of the world's largest parades.

By 1861, there were around 600,000 Irish-born people in Britain. Like many migrant groups, before or since, the Irish tended to live close together in towns and cities. Despite getting work, they were not wealthy, and often ended up in the poorest quality housing in the worst parts of town.

▼ **SOURCE A** *A picture during the potato famine showing a Catholic priest blessing a group of emigrants as they leave Ireland for a new life abroad*

How did the British react to the Irish?

▼ **B** *At the time, many people did not like their new Irish neighbours*

Religious differences

Most of the Irish were Catholic – and Britain was a strongly Protestant country. This was a time when religious differences could lead to violence, and on several occasions angry Protestants marched through Irish areas and destroyed property.

Crime

The Irish were blamed for high crime rates in many towns and cities. The navvies tended to drink a lot and this would sometimes lead to violence. In 1847, *The Times* newspaper described the Irish as 'more like squalid apes than human beings'.

British reaction to the Irish

Disease

The Irish lived in terrible conditions so disease was common. As a result, people would blame the Irish for causing the disease in the first place. The fact that disease was just as common in other places seemed to go unnoticed. Typhus – a deadly infectious disease common in crowded, unsanitary conditions – was even nicknamed 'Irish fever'.

Jobs

The Irish were accused of taking jobs that the British could have done. There were anti-Irish protests; in some places people with Irish accents (or even Irish names) were barred from jobs. As a result, there were times when the Irish couldn't always find regular work – so they were accused of being lazy too.

Key Words

voluntary migration   forced migration   navvy

Impact of Irish migration on Britain

Despite the difficulties, the Irish settlers continued to arrive in Britain, especially in the 1930s, 1950s and 1960s, when people came looking for work in Britain's expanding cities. Over the years there were fewer problems between the Irish and the British as they intermarried. The Irish roots remain strong in places like Liverpool and Birmingham that had a high Irish population in the 1800s. In fact, according to the 2001 census, six million people (ten per cent of the total British population) had Irish parents or grandparents.

The Irish, therefore, have made a huge impact on Britain. Britain's canals, roads and railways could not have been built without the Irish navvies, and in the early 1800s, as many as 40 per cent of soldiers in the British army were Irish. Irish dancing, music and bars have become part of British culture. Famous Irish-born people include writers Oscar Wilde and C. S. Lewis, explorer Ernest Shackleton and the military hero, the Duke of Wellington.

Work

1 a Explain the difference between voluntary and forced migration.
   b Do you think the Irish migrants to Britain experienced voluntary or forced migration, or a mixture of both? Explain your answer carefully.
   c Why did so many people leave Ireland in the 1800s?
2 a Make a list of all the problems blamed on the Irish when they arrived in Britain.
   b Why do you think so many British people were so keen to blame the Irish for their problems?

Practice Question

Explain two ways in which the Huguenot migration to Britain and the Irish migration to Britain were similar.   **8 marks**

Extension

Carry out some additional research into the impact that Irish immigration has had on Britain. Which famous Britons have Irish ancestry? In what ways have the Irish influenced British culture?

Study Tip

Try to write about the contribution each group made to Britain after they arrived.

Jewish migration to Britain

In 1290, as a result of religious intolerance, King Edward I expelled all the Jews from England. It was over 350 years until England's leaders allowed Jews back in. There were only about 400 Jews living in England in 1690. However, by 1850 the number of Jews had grown to about 40,000 (out of a population of 18 million). As the Jewish communities prospered, their contribution to British life grew. Why does Britain have a large Jewish community? And what is their contribution to British society?

Objectives

▶ **Explain** why there was an influx of Jews into Britain in the late 1800s.

▶ **Examine** how Jews were received in Britain at that time.

▶ **Assess** the Jewish contribution to the British way of life.

By the mid-1800s, Jewish people had made important contributions to Britain. The vast majority had been born in Britain, spoke English and lived typical British lifestyles. The first Jewish Mayor of London took office in 1855, and shortly afterwards Lionel de Rothschild became the first Jewish MP. As well as his role as a politician, Rothschild was a banker who famously lent money to the British government to buy a controlling share in the Suez Canal from Egypt. Since then, the British parliament has never been without Jewish politicians. In 1874, Benjamin Disraeli became Britain's first Jewish Prime Minister.

New Jewish migration

In the 1870s and 1880s, there was a new influx of Jews from Eastern Europe, mainly from Russia. Jews were a minority group in Russia and persecution of the Jewish community was commonplace. As a result, Jews had been wrongly blamed for the assassination of the Russian emperor Tsar Alexander II in 1881, and from 1882 a series of laws against them were strictly enforced. There were restrictions placed on the number of Jews allowed in schools, for example, and in some cities like Moscow (in 1891) Jews were expelled altogether. Religious attacks, called **pogroms**, were common too. In 1903, for example, a pogrom in Kishinev (then part of Russia) left 49 Jews dead, 500 injured and hundreds of homes and businesses destroyed. As a result, between 1881 and 1914 around 120,000 Jews arrived in Britain, mainly fleeing from extreme persecution like this.

However, apart from their faith, these new **refugees** had little in common with the Jews already living in Britain. They looked different, were largely uneducated and didn't speak any English. They worked hard but generally lived in the poorest areas. They were badly paid but were charged high rents for their overcrowded, disease-ridden rooms. As more Jews arrived, anger and hostility towards them grew, mainly because they were accused of taking jobs from British workers. This has been a familiar theme – like other new immigrant groups, the Jews were unfairly targeted.

The new immigrants mainly took on three kinds of work – making clothes, shoemaking or furniture-making. These jobs mainly took place in small, back-street workshops, known as 'sweatshops' because of the warm conditions and long hours. But the Jews did very well in their new trades.

Key Biography

Benjamin Disraeli (1804–81)

- Born into a Jewish family, but was baptised as a Christian in 1817.
- Became Prime Minister of Britain twice (in 1868 and again in 1874).
- Arranged for Queen Victoria to be officially titled 'Empress of India' in 1877.

▼ SOURCE A *Disraeli and Queen Victoria, painted in 1887*

Within a few decades, Jewish communities gained a reputation as hardworking, law-abiding citizens. One immigrant called Michael Marks opened a market stall in 1894. His business partner was Tom Spencer, an Englishman. By 1900, Marks & Spencer had 36 outlets, and it is now one of the best-known high street stores in the world. Jack Cohen, the son of Jewish immigrants from Poland, set up a business selling (among other things) tea from a supplier called T. E. Stockwell. He soon created a brand name for his business by using part of his surname and the initials of his main supplier, and TESCO was born.

▼ **SOURCE B** *An engraving of Wentworth Street in Whitechapel, a poor area of London, in 1872. It shows not only poor Jews, but other immigrants – Irish, Indians and Germans, for example.*

Fact

Many people were concerned about the influx of Jews from Eastern Europe. A campaign to stop Jewish immigration began in the late 1800s and continued for many years, despite the fact that many Jews worked incredibly hard and set up shops and businesses in Britain. A number of key politicians supported the campaign, and in 1905 the first Aliens Act was passed by parliament, limiting the number of Jewish immigrants.

Key Words

pogrom   refugee   chain migration

Our 'oldest ethnic minority'

The Jewish community is now a successful and important part of British society. Jews live all over Britain but have particularly large communities in London, Manchester, Leeds and Glasgow. In 2006, during commemorations of 350 years since Jews were re-admitted into Britain, the then Prime Minister Tony Blair said that the Jewish communities of Britain have shown that 'it is possible to retain a clear faith and a clear identity and, at the same time, be thoroughly British'.

Well-known British Jews include Lord Alan Sugar, Daniel Radcliffe, Orlando Bloom and Matt Lucas. Many Jews have fought for Britain, including poet and soldier Siegfried Sassoon, and six British Jewish soldiers have received the Victoria Cross, the highest award for bravery.

Fact

In many cases, young Jewish men emigrated first, then were followed by their wives and children once they had established a home and a place to live. Older relatives followed later. This is known as **chain migration**.

Work

1   For what reasons did large numbers of Jews arrive in Britain in the 1870s and 1880s?
2   a   Describe how the new Jewish immigrants were treated.
    b   Can you think of reasons why they were treated this way?
3   a   Look carefully at **Source B**. Describe what you see – and then try to explain what you think the artist thought about immigrants.
    b   Discuss in pairs: How useful is **Source B** to a historian studying attitudes towards new immigrants in the late 1800s?

People on the move in nineteenth-century Britain

In the eighteenth and nineteenth centuries, many millions of people moved around the British Empire for different reasons. But it wasn't just within the empire that this migration happened – millions of people moved around Britain too. So where did people move to, and why did people move around Britain so much? How did the British Empire affect migration?

Objectives

▶ **Explore** how the British Empire affected migration, including the migration of Asians to Africa.

▶ **Discover** how Australia became an important part of Britain's justice system.

▶ **Examine** why people moved from rural to urban settings between 1750 and 1900.

During the era of the British Empire, millions of people migrated huge distances across the globe. Some of these people had no choice but to move and were forced to go. Others willingly migrated as they looked for fresh challenges and new opportunities.

Forced migration

Case study: Africa and Asia

The most obvious example of forced migration was the transport of millions of enslaved Africans to work on sugar, tobacco and cotton farms in the Caribbean and North America. The **transportation** of prisoners to America and Australia in the 1700s and 1800s is another example of forced migration.

When slavery ended in the early 1800s, the British needed another way to get large numbers of people to work on their plantations, estates and farms in various parts of the empire. The **indenture system** was created, meaning that migrants would agree to work for a period of five years in return for a basic wage and transport to their new workplace. The worker was to be returned at the end of the period of service to the port of departure. Around half of the immigrants to the American colonies in the sixteenth and seventeenth centuries went there under this system, as did millions of Tamils from South India who went to pick tea on estates in Sri Lanka, or tap rubber in Malaya (now Malaysia). It has been estimated that, between 1841 and 1910, around 150,000 people

per decade moved around the empire under this system. In the British African colonies of Kenya and Uganda, for example, over 30,000 Indians moved there under the indenture system to help build railways, bridges and roads. Some came home when the work was done, but thousands stayed and they and their descendants went on to play a vital part in the African economies as businessmen, bankers, shopkeepers and professionals. By the late 1960s there were about 180,000 'Kenyan Asians' (as they were known) and around 60,000 'Ugandan Asians'.

▼ **SOURCE A** *The 1000-kilometre-long Uganda Railway in British East Africa was built mainly by indentured workers from India, like the ones pictured here*

Key Words

transactions

transportation
indenture system
Aboriginal people

Case study: Australia

In April 1770, a British explorer named James Cook claimed the east coast of Australia for Britain and named it New South Wales. The British government then sent naval commander Captain Arthur Phillip to set up the first colony on Australian soil. The government also wanted him to transport convicts from Britain's overcrowded jails to help him do it: it was hoped that these prisoners would never return to Britain. In May 1787, 11 ships left Portsmouth heading for the new British colony. There were over 1300 people on board the ships, including 736 convicted criminals.

The convicts began to build the settlement. Each convict was assigned a master. The master decided what work each convict would carry out. Good, hardworking convicts earned themselves an early release, while bad behaviour ended in a whipping or an extended sentence. Over the next 20 years, British courts transported over 20,000 more convicts to join them. But life in the new settlement was tough. Few of the convicts – or their masters – knew about farming or carpentry, two of the most important skills needed in the new colony.

Australia was first used mainly as a place to dump Britain's criminals, but things

Fact

Transportation became a very common punishment. It not only removed the criminal from Britain, but it was also quite cheap: the government only had to pay the cost of a one-way journey. The punishment began in the 1600s when the British colonies in North America began to receive transported British criminals. This stopped when the American War of Independence broke out in 1775; Australia then became the favoured alternative destination after 1787.

▼ **SOURCE B** *The first British colony in Australia, pictured around 1835. It was named Sydney after a British politician. Note the **Aboriginal** Australians fishing in the bay. The term 'Aboriginal' is from the Latin* ab *(meaning from) and* origo *(meaning beginning).*

soon started to change. The majority of convicts decided to stay in Australia at the end of their sentences. Many became sheep or wheat farmers. Britain would eventually claim the whole of Australia as part of the British Empire.

Work

1 What is the difference between 'forced migration' and the 'indenture system'?
2 What work did people who were forced to migrate to Africa and Australia do?
3 What happened to them and their descendants?

Extension

Try to find out what happened to some of Australia's convicts. For example some, upon their release after their sentences, became famous artists, architects and merchants. One former convict earned enough money to help pay for the building of one of Australia's most famous schools.

People on the move in nineteenth-century Britain

Leaving home

It has been estimated that over 22 million people left Britain between 1815 and 1914, the vast majority going to North America, South Africa, Canada, Australia and New Zealand. They left hoping to make a better life for themselves in a country where they felt they had more opportunities. They did all sorts of jobs when they got to their destinations. Most men found work in building, engineering, farming or mining, while women took up jobs as tutors or maids. Thousands were lured to North America and South Africa to hunt for gold and diamonds. In the late 1700s, the first 'free settlers' began to arrive in Australia from Britain, attracted by the idea of a new life in another part of the world. They brought the supplies and skills needed to help the settlement survive and grow.

Emigration was also seen as a solution to the growing problem of crime and poverty in Britain. The government gave local councils money to create schemes that encouraged the poorest people in an area to emigrate. Other schemes took young criminals away from their families and set them up in new lives in Canada or Australia.

Moving around Britain

Migration is not just about leaving one country to go to another. A person can also migrate *within* their own country. This is sometimes called **internal migration**. This took place in Britain, more rapidly than at any other time, between 1750 and 1900.

During this period, the population of Britain rose quickly. Better medical treatments, improved food supplies and improved sanitation are among some of the many reasons why more people survived childhood and lived longer lives. In fact, Britain's population went from around 10 million in 1801 to about 37 million in 1901.

The number of people in towns and cities (**urban** areas) grew much faster than in country (**rural**) areas at this time, particularly in London and the large industrial towns in the north and the Midlands. In 1750, for

example, around 80 per cent of people lived and worked in the countryside. By 1825, this had dropped to 60 per cent, and by 1901 around 75 per cent of people lived and worked in towns and cities. We call this process **urbanisation** – the increase in the proportion of people living in urban areas. There were several reasons why towns and industrial areas grew more rapidly than country areas:

- Immigration from abroad: immigrants were attracted to jobs in urban areas. Many workers came from Ireland, for example, to find jobs in the cotton mills of Lancashire and Yorkshire. By 1851, 10 per cent of the population of Manchester and 15 per cent of the population of Liverpool were of Irish origin. In Coatbridge, a mining town near Glasgow, the Irish proportion of the population was 49 per cent.
- Rural to urban migration: farm machinery became more common, so fewer workers were needed on farms. Farming is also very seasonal, whereas factory work isn't, so workers in the countryside poured into urban areas to find work. The larger the towns became, the more jobs this created in shops, businesses, building work and so on.

▼ **C** *Population of two English counties (in thousands)*

County	Main job type	1701	1751	1781	1801
Lancashire	Industrial	239	318	423	694
Suffolk	Farming	161	159	188	217

Extension

Research what the 'push' and 'pull' factors of migration are. Then carry out a survey of the people in your class to establish the levels of internal migration and immigration. What were the push and pull factors in each case? How do the push and pull factors from those moving *around* the UK (internal migration) compare to those moving *into* the UK (immigration)?

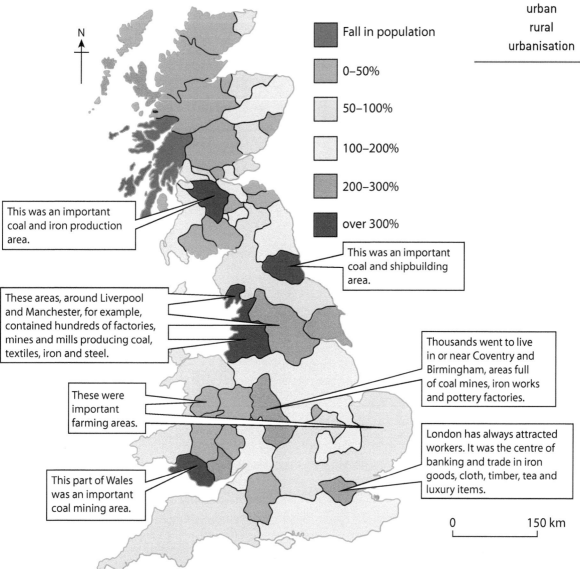

▼ **D** *A map showing the regional population increase in Britain from 1801 to 1871, and the types of jobs and industry in particular areas*

N

Fall in population

0–50%

50–100%

100–200%

200–300%

over 300%

This was an important coal and iron production area.

This was an important coal and shipbuilding area.

These areas, around Liverpool and Manchester, for example, contained hundreds of factories, mines and mills producing coal, textiles, iron and steel.

Thousands went to live in or near Coventry and Birmingham, areas full of coal mines, iron works and pottery factories.

These were important farming areas.

London has always attracted workers. It was the centre of banking and trade in iron goods, cloth, timber, tea and luxury items.

This part of Wales was an important coal mining area.

0   150 km

Work

1 Give three examples of how different people might have moved around the British Empire.

2 a Explain what is meant by the term 'urbanisation'.

 b What were the main causes of urbanisation between 1750 and 1900?

3 Look at table **C**. Why was the population increase so much greater in one county than the other?

4 Look at map **D**. Explain why the populations of Manchester and Liverpool increased far more rapidly than the populations of mid-Wales.

Practice Question

Has industrialisation been the main factor causing changes in the population of Britain in the nineteenth century?   **16 marks**

SPaG: 4 marks

Study Tip

Consider the push and pull factors involved in causing people to move.

How and why did the British Empire end?

Map A below shows the British Empire at its largest, in the early 1920s. At that point it was the largest empire the world had ever known. It contained around 450 million people (approximately one quarter of the world's population) and it covered about one quarter of the world's total land area. Today the British Empire (now called the British Overseas Territories) is very small, consisting of a few small areas, mainly islands, dotted around the world. At its height, the empire covered around 34 million square kilometres. Today, it covers around 1.7 million square kilometres. What happened to the British Empire?

Objectives

▶ **Recall** how Britain gradually lost its empire.

▶ **Evaluate** the impact of the First and Second World Wars and the Suez Crisis on the decline of the British Empire.

▶ **Assess** the importance of independence and nationalism, as well as the roles of Gandhi, Nkrumah and Kenyatta, in the empire's decline.

▼ **A** *The British Empire at its territorial peak in 1921*

The impact of the world wars

Before the First World War, Britain was one of the richest countries in the world, with its mighty industrial power and vast empire. However, after four years of fighting, Britain's wealth was nearly all gone: it was now in debt because it had borrowed money, mainly from the USA. Also, during the war many countries had been cut off from the supply of British goods so had been forced to build up their own industries. They were no longer reliant on Britain, and directly competed with it instead. The First World War changed Britain's status in the world: it was no longer the world's economic superpower.

After the war, Britain recovered some of its strength, but it was then completely bankrupted by the Second World War. Britain's economy was also beginning to change. Its trade with Europe and the USA became far more important than its trade with countries of the empire. Britain was also no longer as important on the world stage. It was now overshadowed by the political and financial might of the USA and the Soviet Union.

Demanding independence

By 1914, several of Britain's colonies – such as Canada, Australia, New Zealand and South Africa – had already been running their own affairs for several years. In 1922, Egypt became independent too. Some critics of British rule suggested that Britain was more comfortable to allow self-rule in countries that contained a majority of white settlers (such as Australia and Canada) rather than 'non-white' colonies such as India or in Africa. They suggested that the British thought people of European descent were superior to non-Europeans.

Many countries in the empire, including former colonies, played an important role in Britain's victory in both world wars by supplying troops and materials. However, by the end of the Second World War, many other British colonies were demanding independence, or the right to rule themselves. Britain no longer had the military strength or the wealth to hold onto them. Also, many British people felt that rebuilding Britain after the war was far more of a priority than holding on to distant colonies.

There were several reasons why there was an increasing demand for independence:

- Education systems improved at that time in some colonies, such as India, which meant that many more people there were now becoming teachers, lawyers and doctors. They learned about political ideas, like democracy, freedom and **nationalism**. This meant that many people in these colonies wanted these things for their own countries. In India and other non-white colonies (such as Jamaica), the demand for independence was very strong.

- The Africans and Indians who had fought for Britain felt they were fighting to defend freedom, and were getting increasingly frustrated that their own countries were not yet free. They thought it was wrong that they should fight to stop the Nazis occupying other countries, but not fight to stop Britain occupying theirs.
- Researchers and historians were showing how important the cultures and achievements of Africa and Asia had been before the Europeans took over. Many people in the colonies wanted to celebrate their own traditions, and this could only be done if the British left.

After the Second World War, Britain lost its empire very quickly. It had taken centuries to build up, but only decades to lose.

Case study: independence for India

The campaign for Indian independence began with the founding of the **Indian National Congress** in 1885, which held meetings and organised demonstrations, although the British largely ignored their demands. In 1919, after India's great contribution in the First World War, the British made slight changes to the way India was governed. Law-making councils were set up in each province and over five million wealthy Indians were given the vote. However, the British government in London still controlled taxation, the armed forces, education and much more.

In the 1920s, the Indian independence movement gained more support under the leadership of Mohandas Gandhi, a Hindu and former lawyer. He led a series of non-violent protests against the British. Eventually, in 1935, the Government of India Act gave Indians the right to control everything except the army. But India was still part of the British Empire and was still ruled by a viceroy. Many Indians, like Gandhi, continued to demand complete independence. By now, Muslims in India had formed their own independence group (the **Muslim League**), and their leader called for a new separate country for Muslims.

Key Words

nationalism   Indian National Congress
Muslim League   partition

Work

1 Compare the British Empire at its height with the British Overseas Territories today.

2 Why did some colonies begin to demand their independence from Britain?

3 Why do you think some critics of the British Empire accused the British of racist attitudes when it came to allowing some countries to rule themselves?

Extension

GCSE

Mohandas Gandhi (1869–1948) was a famous leader who used non-violence as a means to make a difference. Conduct research into his life and write a short 'Key Biography' of his achievements.

After the Second World War, Britain wasn't strong enough to hold on to a country so determined to rule itself. In 1946, Britain offered independence to India – but Muslims did not want to live under a Hindu majority and terrible violence broke out. Indian and British leaders finally agreed to **partition** British India into two states – Hindu India and Muslim Pakistan. Pakistan became independent on 14 August 1947, and India the next day. Immediately, over seven million Muslims fled to Pakistan, and the same number of Hindus and Sikhs fled to India, and violence occurred. Sadly, troubles at the start of the two new, independent nations continue to this day.

▼ **SOURCE B** *Gandhi standing in front of 10 Downing Street with British Prime Minister Ramsay MacDonald, 1931*

The Suez Crisis

After Indian independence, the next blow to Britain's empire was the Suez Crisis. In 1956, Egypt's President Nasser took control of the British- and French-owned Suez Canal. The canal was valuable to Britain as a gateway to the Middle East. When talks failed, British and French troops landed in the canal zone, and Israel, an ally of the two countries, attacked Egypt overland. The whole world was shocked, and both the USA and the United Nations condemned the invasion. The troops were forced to withdraw and Britain's Prime Minister resigned in humiliation.

The impact of the crisis was clear — Britain could no longer go to war to preserve its interests if the rest of the world disapproved. As a result, the British decided to allow independence in colonies they felt were stable and prosperous enough to run their own affairs. They hoped that by freely granting independence, they were more likely to have a successful relationship with the newly formed countries.

Case study: independence along the African Gold Coast

Europeans had been trading both gold and enslaved people along the west coast of Africa since the 1500s. Because of its gold mines, the area became known as the Gold Coast. In 1874, the British officially took control of the Gold Coast during the 'scramble for Africa'.

In the 1920s, an independence campaign began in West Africa. A number of educated West Africans created the **National Congress of British West Africa** and asked the British government for more control of their own affairs, but the request was rejected. By the 1940s, there were large independence movements in several African nations including Nigeria, Gold Coast, Sierra Leone and The Gambia.

After the Second World War, the British were not against independence for West African countries, but felt it was important that any new countries in the region were stable and democratic.

The Gold Coast was one of the most stable and prosperous countries in the region. Its key independence leader, Dr Kwame Nkrumah, campaigned hard for the British to leave and was thrown in jail several times by the British colonial authorities. In the 1951 elections, Nkrumah won, even though he was still in jail. The British let him out of prison and he was allowed to become Prime Minister — but the Gold Coast remained part of the British Empire. In 1956, he was re-elected, and the British took this as a sign that they should leave. The Gold Coast became the independent state of Ghana in March 1957.

Key Biography

Kwame Nkrumah (1909–72)

- Spent time studying at universities in both the USA and Britain.
- Returned to the Gold Coast to begin his political career in 1946.
- Wrote his first book on independence in Africa in 1947, called *Towards Colonial Freedom*.
- Had a troubled time as Ghana's leader. Ghana became a republic in 1960, and Nkrumah was elected President. There were fierce rivalries between him and other political leaders and there was an attempted assassination in 1962.
- He dealt harshly with groups that opposed his rule. The economy declined in the early 1960s and the army and the police seized control in 1966. Nkrumah fled to nearby Guinea and later Romania.

▼ SOURCE C   *Kwame Nkrumah visiting Balmoral Castle in Scotland in August 1959, pictured with Queen Elizabeth II and Princess Anne*

Case study: independence in Kenya

In Kenya, a number of groups formed to fight for self-rule in the 1940s. One group, the **Kenya African Union** (KAU) and its leader Jomo Kenyatta, campaigned for both independence and access to white-owned land. Another group, known as the Mau Mau, favoured violence against the white settlers who controlled large areas of land. In the 1950s, the British fought the Mau Mau with their own violent campaign and hundreds were killed. Many Kenyan independence leaders (including those with no connection to the Mau Mau, such as Kenyatta) were arrested and jailed. Many white settlers later chose to leave Kenya.

The **Mau Mau Rebellion**, as it was known, lasted for over eight years and eventually persuaded the British that reforms were necessary. On 12 December 1963, Kenya gained its independence from Britain, and Kenyatta, who had been released from prison in 1961, became Prime Minister.

In 2013, the British government apologised for the way it had dealt with the Mau Mau Rebellion and agreed to pay compensation.

Key Words

National Congress of British West Africa
Kenya African Union   Mau Mau Rebellion

Key Biography

Jomo Kenyatta (1891–1978)

- After working as an apprentice carpenter, became involved in the Kenyan independence movement.
- In 1947, was elected President of the Kenya African Union (KAU) and campaigned for independence.
- Was accused of being a member of the Mau Mau and imprisoned from 1953 to 1961.
- Became Kenya's Prime Minister (1963) and later President (1964). He dealt harshly with groups that opposed his rule – and eventually banned opposition parties.

▶ **SOURCE D**
Jomo Kenyatta celebrating Kenya's independence from Britain in 1963

Work

1 a Describe the Suez Crisis.
  b What was the impact of the Suez Crisis on Britain and its empire?

2 Look again at the Gold Coast and Kenya case studies. Make a list of similarities and differences between the ways in which these nations gained independence.

Practice Question

Were the two world wars the main factors in causing Britain to lose much of its empire in the twentieth century?

16 marks
SPaG: 4 marks

Study Tip

Plan your answer to have at least two paragraphs. One should be on the world wars and a second on another important factor.

Why did immigrants come to Britain after the Second World War?

11.1

There were two main reasons why large groups of immigrants came to Britain after 1945. Some arrived as refugees from war-torn Europe. Their homes and livelihoods had been destroyed so many looked for a new life and new opportunities in Britain. Other migrants came from parts of the British Empire to find work. The government encouraged migration because there was a shortage of workers, particularly in mining, building, transport, healthcare and farming. The map on these pages outlines some of the main areas where these immigrants came from in the years immediately after the war. It also details locations where people have moved from in later years.

Objectives

▶ **Explain** where the majority of immigrants to Britain after the Second World War have migrated from.

▶ **Examine** the reasons why these people migrated to Britain.

Ireland

Many generations of Irish people had come to Britain before 1945. There were further surges of Irish immigration in the 1950s and 1960s. Some came to join their families in existing communities, and others came to look for work in Britain's expanding cities, and to escape poverty and hardship in Ireland. By the 1960s, the number of people of Irish origin in Britain had risen to nearly one million. And by 2001, around six million people (ten per cent of the total British population) had Irish parents or grandparents.

The Caribbean

During the Second World War, thousands of people from the Caribbean moved to Britain to help with the war effort, although most returned home when the fighting ended. From 1948 to 1970, many more people (around half a million) from the colonies of Jamaica, Barbados, and Trinidad and Tobago were encouraged to come to Britain because of the labour shortage. Many came because of unemployment and poverty at home too.

The Caribbean

Cyprus

Cyprus became a British colony after the First World War. Both Turkish and Greek people lived on the island. They had different cultures and languages and there was often tension and violence between the two groups. Thousands of Cypriots fled the violence (as well as poverty and hardship) to start a new life in Britain in the 1950s. The island became an independent country in 1960, but when Turkey invaded and divided the island in two in the 1970s, there was a further period of emigration when around 70,000 Cypriots left to make their home in Britain.

Europe

By the start of the twentieth century, around 200,000 Eastern European Jews had fled persecution and settled in Britain. In the 1930s, around 60,000 German Jews came to Britain when the Nazis gained power. When fighting broke out in 1939, thousands of Poles sought safety in Britain, and when the war ended around 114,000 of them decided not to return to Poland. By 1950, around 100,000 Hungarians, Ukrainians, Yugoslavs, Estonians, Latvians and Lithuanians who had fled from Russian rule had also settled in Britain.

East Asia

People from East Asia began to move to Britain during the 1950s and 1960s. Most came from the poorest areas of the British colony of Hong Kong, but others came from British-controlled Malaysia and Singapore. By 1961, there were around 30,000 people from East Asia living in Britain. In 1997, Hong Kong stopped being a British colony and became part of China. Around 50,000 people from Hong Kong were given British passports at this time. Today there are around 400,000 British Chinese people.

South Asia

When India gained independence from Britain in 1947, it split into different countries: India and Pakistan. This partition led to fighting, as whole populations moved across the dividing lines. Some came to Britain to escape this violence. By 1955, around 10,000 people had moved to Britain, hoping to find work and better education opportunities. Many started their own businesses or worked in industries like textiles or steel making. Today around four million people of South Asian descent live in Britain.

Extension

People don't just move *into* Britain. British people also move abroad. Research the most popular destinations for British people moving abroad today.

Work

1 Make a list of all the reasons why different groups have moved to Britain. You might want to divide your list into 'push' and 'pull' factors: push factors are reasons why people are driven away from their own countries, and pull factors are reasons why people are attracted to life in Britain.

2 In groups or in pairs, discuss what you think were the most common reasons why people came to Britain.

3 Can you make a link between immigration to Britain and the British Empire? Explain your answer.

West Africa

The countries of British West Africa (now Nigeria, The Gambia, Sierra Leone and Ghana) made a huge contribution in the Second World War. They provided soldiers, raw materials and air bases. After 1948, many West Africans went to Britain to find employment and to get a better standard of education than was available in their own countries.

Kenya and Uganda

Around 70,000 Kenyan and Ugandan Asians moved to Britain from their homes in Africa in the 1960s and 1970s. They had originally moved to Africa from India and Pakistan, when these nations were part of the British Empire, to build railways and roads. Most stayed, and made strong communities. By the twentieth century, they played a vital part in the economies there, as shopkeepers and professionals. But when Kenya and Uganda became independent from Britain, the new governments decided to drive them out, so many came to Britain to escape racist attitudes and intolerance. In Uganda, President Idi Amin told Ugandan Asians to leave the country, after he claimed he'd had a dream in which God told him to expel them! Jomo Kenyatta, the Kenyan leader, introduced a law that banned Kenyan Asians from trading in certain areas. Around 44,000 Asians from Kenya and 26,000 from Uganda came to Britain at this time.

Empire Windrush and the Caribbean migrants

On 22 June 1948, a ship named *Empire Windrush* arrived at the London docks. The ship was returning to London from Australia and had stopped off in Kingston, Jamaica, to pick up British soldiers who were there on leave. But it wasn't just soldiers who got on the ship in Jamaica: 492 other people did too, most of them young men, who were travelling to Britain to start a new life. This was an event that would change the face of British society forever. Why did these newcomers move to Britain in the first place? How were they, and others who followed in later years, treated?

Objectives

▶ **Define** the 'Commonwealth' and consider why Commonwealth migrants from the Caribbean decided to move to Britain.

▶ **Discover** what life was like for the 'Windrush generation' when they arrived in Britain.

▶ **Assess** the impact of the Windrush generation, including the role of Claudia Jones.

▼ **SOURCE A** *The* Empire Windrush *at Tilbury docks, London; the first black immigrants to arrive in Britain from the Caribbean after the Second World War became known as the 'Windrush generation'*

At the time of the Second World War, many islands in the Caribbean Sea (known then as the British West Indies) were part of the British Empire, including Jamaica, Barbados, and Trinidad and Tobago. These islands had supplied over 10,000 men for Britain's army, navy and air force, and they had been proud of their role in helping Britain. However, soon after the fighting ended and they returned home, they found they had little to celebrate. Life was very hard in the Caribbean in the 1940s. Jamaica had been devastated by a hurricane in 1944, and poverty and hardship were common. The Caribbean had not yet developed a tourist industry to provide jobs, and the price of sugar – the Caribbean's main export and source of income – was at an all-time low. To ambitious men seeking better opportunities and wanting to see the country they had been fighting for, it was clear that their future lay abroad in Britain, the 'mother country'.

▼ **SOURCE B** *Ulric Cross was one of 250 Trinidadians who joined the RAF when the Second World War broke out; he flew over 80 bombing missions, 20 of them over Germany*

The Commonwealth

In 1948, the British parliament passed the British Nationality Act. This meant that all people who lived within the British Empire – now commonly referred to as the **Commonwealth** – were British passport holders and therefore entitled to live and work in Britain. Many African Caribbeans saw this as a great opportunity.

Having been brought up speaking English, named after British heroes, and educated to believe in 'king and country', many African Caribbeans felt very 'British'. And at the time, Britain was short of workers, for example in transport, healthcare and building.

Fact

Nearly all former colonies of the British Empire now belong to an organisation called 'The Commonwealth of Nations'. It promotes democracy, human rights, good government, fair laws and world peace in the nations that were formerly controlled by Britain. There are currently 54 member countries (containing 1.7 billion people – 30 per cent of the world's population), each with close cultural, trade and sporting links to Britain.

▼ **SOURCE C** *Adapted from an article in* The Guardian *newspaper, 23 June 1948; the term 'coloured' was used at the time to describe black people, but it is considered offensive today*

What manner of men are these the *Empire Windrush* has brought to Britain? This morning, on the decks, I spoke with the following: an apprentice accountant, a farm worker, a tailor, a boxer, a mechanic, a singer, and a law student. Or thus they described themselves.

And what had made them leave Jamaica? In most cases, lack of work. Most of the married men have left their wives and children at home, and hope to send for them later.

They are, then, as mixed a collection of humanity as one might find. Some will be good workers, some bad. No doubt the singers will find audiences somewhere. Not all intend to settle in Britain; a 40-year-old tailor, for example, hopes to stay here for a year, and then go on and make his home in Africa.

But the more world-wise among them are conscious of the deeper problem posed. In the past Britain has welcomed displaced persons who cannot go home. 'This is right,' said one of the immigrants. 'Surely then, there is nothing against our coming, for we are British subjects. If there is – is it because we are coloured?'

Key Word

Commonwealth

▼ **SOURCE D** *Prize-winning student nurses at the Dreadnought Seamen's Hospital in 1954: C. S. Ramsay of Jamaica (left), C. Bishop of England (centre) and J. E. Samuel of Trinidad (right)*

Work

1 a List reasons why many people wanted to leave the Caribbean at the end of the Second World War.
   b List reasons why people from the Caribbean may have chosen to come to Britain.
2 What was the British Nationality Act?
3 a What was the *Empire Windrush*?
   b Find at least two reasons contained in **Source C** that explain why some of the passengers on the ship came to Britain.

Practice Question

How useful is **Source C** to a historian studying the reaction in Britain to Caribbean migrants?

8 marks

Study Tip

What do you think is the attitude of the journalist to the migrants?

Empire Windrush and the Caribbean migrants

Impact of *Empire Windrush*

The voyage of the *Empire Windrush* made headlines before the ship had even arrived. Thousands of immigrants from Europe had been coming to Britain ever since the Second World War finished, but it was the arrival of this ship of English-speaking, Christian, British citizens that made the headlines. Newspapers were full of stories of the 'colour problem' that was heading towards Britain, and some politicians demanded that the ship should be turned around and sent back. When the ship finally docked, the smartly dressed Caribbean migrants smiled nervously at the journalists, and one of them sang a song called 'London's the Place for Me'. Soon, most had found jobs – and their friends and relatives followed in search of work.

▼ **SOURCE E** *Some of the men from the* Empire Windrush, *dressed in their best suits, photographed on arrival in London on 22 June 1948; pictures like these have come to symbolise the beginning of Britain's modern multicultural society*

The British experience

Not all white Britons welcomed Britain's newest citizens. Many African Caribbeans found that their skin colour provoked hostile reactions. Some immigrants found good jobs, but many – whatever their qualifications – ended up working in low-paid jobs as cleaners, ticket collectors and hospital porters. They also experienced difficulties finding decent places to live. Often, they would be faced with openly racist words on house rental signs specifying 'No Irish, No Blacks, No dogs'. These racist attitudes that prevented black and other minority ethnic groups from renting houses and getting jobs became known as the '**colour bar**'.

In the 1940s, Caribbean arrivals in Britain numbered around 500 to 700 each year. By 1953, the figure had

▼ **SOURCE F** *Jamaican men in a street in Brixton, south London in the 1950s; the racist graffiti on the wall stands for 'Keep Britain White'*

▼ **SOURCE G** *Sam King, one of the passengers on the* Empire Windrush, *had fought in the RAF during the Second World War and later became the Mayor of Southwark, London. His family sold three cows to buy his ticket for the ship, which cost £28.10s at the time (around £600 today). King said:*

> The second day in Britain I was offered five jobs. If someone wants to leave, let them leave, but I have been here during the war fighting Nazi Germany and I came back and helped build Britain. People said that we would not stay longer than one year; we are here, and I and my people are here to stay.

▼ **SOURCE H** *John Richards, one of the passengers on the* Empire Windrush, *said:*

> I knew a lot about Britain from schooldays, but it was a different picture when you came face to face with the facts. They tell you it is the 'mother country', you're all welcome, you're all British. When you come here you realise you're a foreigner and that's all there is to it.

increased to around 2200 per year. By 1960, there were around 40,000 African-Caribbean immigrants arriving each year. This outnumbered all other immigrants from other areas of the world. The newcomers settled in industrial areas such as Liverpool, Manchester, Birmingham and Nottingham. Most, however, stayed in London.

There were some outbreaks of violence in areas where there were large African-Caribbean populations. In 1958, in Nottingham and in Notting Hill, London, there were several weeks of violence when white youths attacked black youths on the streets, at nightclubs and in their homes. In fact, the Notting Hill Carnival began as a gesture of defiance by the black community against these widespread racial attacks. Some politicians with extreme anti-immigration views gained some support, but racist political parties remained fairly small.

In 1962, the government made an attempt to slow down the number of black and Asian people entering Britain by passing an Immigration Act. This said that any black or Asian person wanting to enter the country must have a skilled job already lined up – and a limit was put on the number of immigrants allowed in. However, no limits were put on Irish immigrants or any other white minority ethnic groups, such as Australians. In 1968, when the government feared a large influx of Kenyan Asians into Britain, the Commonwealth Immigration Act was created. This said that Kenyan Asians with British passports were no longer allowed to enter the country – but white Kenyans with British passports were! These policies divided the country. They were welcomed by those who were not happy with the large number of immigrants coming into the country, while others felt that that the laws were racist. Yet despite the discrimination, the racial tension and other obstacles, thousands of people from the Caribbean decided to make Britain their home.

Key Words

colour bar   asylum

Work

1   Why might people from the Caribbean believe they had a right to move to Britain?

2   Use all the information and sources on pages 84–87 to answer the following question: Who were the 'Windrush generation' and what was life like for them in 1940s and 1950s Britain?

3   The Caribbean migrants on the *Empire Windrush* moved to a completely new country, with a different climate and culture. How might they have felt about moving and what do you think they would like or dislike about their new home? Discuss with a partner your own experiences of moving to a new house, or a new school. Do you think our experiences help us to understand the experiences of the *Empire Windrush* immigrants?

Key Biography

Claudia Jones (1915–64)

- Born in Trinidad, moved to New York as a child.

- Worked on newspapers and magazines; championed democracy, equal rights for African Americans, and safe working conditions.

- Was considered an extreme radical in America because of her views and was deported; gained **asylum** in Britain in 1955.

- In 1958, became founder and editor of the first black British weekly newspaper, *The West Indian Gazette*, which she used in her fight for equality.

- Following the Notting Hill and Nottingham riots in 1958, she helped launch an annual 'Mardi Gras' event in 1959, aimed at showing the culture and talent of the Caribbean to the people of Britain. She said she wanted to 'wash the taste of Notting Hill and Nottingham out of our mouths'. This later became the Notting Hill Carnival, one of the largest street festivals in the world.

Extension

Carry out your own research on Claudia Jones. Spend some time finding out about her early life, focusing on the things that might have influenced her in her younger years. Then think about this question: What is the significance of Claudia Jones on the legacy of the British Empire?

What was the significance of the Falklands War?

Over the last hundred years, the British Empire has gradually got smaller as more countries have begun to rule themselves. However, several small colonies dotted around the world did not leave and remain part of the British Empire. One of these colonies is a group of islands in the southern Atlantic Ocean, off the east coast of Argentina, called the Falkland Islands. In 1982, Britain fought a war to defend these islands when Argentina invaded. Why did the war happen, and what were the key events? What impact did the war have on Britain and its position on the world stage?

Objectives

▶ **Outline** the causes of the Falklands War.

▶ **Examine** the key events of the war.

▶ **Evaluate** the impact of the war.

The Falklands are located about 480 kilometres off the coast of Argentina. They are a collection of over 700 islands, but most people live on the two main islands, East and West Falkland. Britain first claimed the islands in 1765, but the Spanish later took them over and named them the Islas Malvinas. When Spanish rule ended in 1806, the islands were claimed by Argentina. Up to this point, the islands were uninhabited. Britain seized the islands from Argentina in 1833, and British settlers began to live there. As a result, the majority of the population of around 2000 are of British descent. From the time that Britain took control of the islands there has been a long, heated argument between Argentina and Britain over who should control them.

What caused the Falklands War in 1982?

In the early 1980s, Argentina was controlled by the army and its leader, General Galtieri. Argentina's economy was having severe problems at this time – unemployment was high, banks were failing and prices were rising quickly. Galtieri hoped that a quick, successful war that ended with the return of the Falklands to Argentina would take people's minds off their problems and restore their belief in him.

On 2 April 1982, Argentine troops invaded the islands. About 12,000 soldiers arrived, and they quickly took control. Most South American countries (except Colombia and Chile) supported Argentina's invasion and its claim to the islands. However, most of Argentina's troops were new recruits who were poorly trained.

Britain's Prime Minister, Margaret Thatcher, responded quickly and defiantly to the invasion. She said, 'We have to recover those islands. We have to recover them for the people on them are British and British stock and they still owe allegiance to the Crown and want to be British.' She received near universal support from politicians and the British public, and plans to re-take the Falklands were up and running very soon.

Britain sent a **task force** of over 100 ships and around 28,000 troops to the islands, and declared a 320-kilometre **exclusion zone** around them. This meant that the British would, without any warning, open fire on any ship or aircraft from any country entering the zone. Britain and Argentina were now at war, which ended on 14 June when the Argentines surrendered. In total, about 750 Argentines and 255 British troops were killed during the war.

▼ **SOURCE A** *British soldiers flying the British flag at Port Howard, West Falkland, June 1982; at the same time another flag was flown at Port Stanley, signifying the end of the war*

▼ **SOURCE B** *The route of the British task force and the exclusion zone. HMS* Sheffield *was a British ship, and the* General Belgrano *was an Argentinian ship. As well as the Falklands, Argentina also attacked the British-controlled islands of South Georgia and the South Sandwich Islands.*

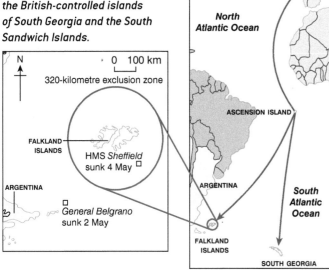

The impact of the Falklands War

The war cost Britain the lives of 255 men, six ships (ten others were damaged), 34 aircraft and over £2.5 billion. Politically, however, the war was a huge boost to the popularity of the British Prime Minister, Margaret Thatcher. Before the war Thatcher was heavily criticised because unemployment was high, some British industries were struggling, and the government had cut spending significantly. The British victory in the war played a role in her re-election in 1983.

The relationship between Britain and the USA became stronger during the conflict too, with US President Ronald Reagan even offering to loan Britain a US warship if a British aircraft carrier was sunk. This 'special relationship' between Britain and the USA has remained in place ever since.

There was also a boost in patriotic feeling among British citizens, who were proud of their country's defence of one of its last colonies. Foreign politicians reported that there was an increase in international respect for Britain, a country that was regarded as a fading power after the failure of the 1956 Suez campaign and the loss of its colonies. In 2012, a commemorative service was held to mark the thirtieth anniversary of the start of the war. The British Prime Minister, David Cameron, said, 'We are rightly proud of the role Britain played in righting a profound wrong. And the people of the Falkland Islands can be justly proud of the prosperous and secure future they have built for

Key Words

task force

exclusion zone

their islands since 1982.' The war even had a positive effect in Argentina. After the country's humiliating loss, President Galtieri was forced to resign, paving the way for a new, democratic government in 1983.

However, the war did not end the dispute between the two countries. Argentina continues to claim the islands, but Britain maintains that this is not open to negotiation. To this day, the Argentinians always refer to the islands as Islas Malvinas. Around 1000 British troops are posted there and are involved in patrolling the islands, as well as road building and monitoring the huge quantity of explosive mines that were planted there by Argentine forces during the conflict.

Work

1 Why did Argentina invade the Falklands? Try to think about both long-term and short-term reasons in your answer.

2 Look at **Source A**. Why do you think this image appeared in newspapers across the country – and the world – shortly after Britain's victory?

3 In your own words, explain the impact of the war on: Margaret Thatcher; Britain's relationship with the USA; Britain's status in the world; Argentina.

Practice Question

Explain two ways in which Britain's reaction to the invasion of the Falklands and the seizure of the Suez Canal were different.

8 marks

Study Tip

Read pages 80–81 to recall what happened with the Suez Canal crisis. You could consider in your response how the outcome of each event was different.

12.1 What is Britain's relationship with Europe?

During the first half of the twentieth century, Western Europe was devastated by the two world wars. During the second half of the century, Europe witnessed increased stability and wealth, and closer cooperation than ever before. Why did Europe become largely peaceful? What are the advantages and disadvantages of European unity and cooperation for Britain?

After the horrors of the Second World War, when European neighbours were enemies, European leaders saw that things had to change. They were determined to avoid another large-scale war, and felt that future peace was far more likely if differences in language, culture and history were put aside, and countries worked together. Rather than compete as rivals, they would join forces where possible to develop Europe peacefully. Also, it was thought that a strong, unified Europe might become a powerful trading group and a competitor for the increasingly powerful and influential USA.

The early years

To begin with, Britain didn't join either the **European Coal and Steel Community (ECSC)** or the **European Economic Community (EEC)**. At this time Britain had strong ties with countries that were still part of the British Empire, and also with those that had gained independence. Britain was also closely linked with the USA. However, in the early 1960s, things began to change. Many more countries began to gain their independence from Britain and it was clear that the EEC was becoming an economic success. Britain's first

Timeline

1951	1957	1968	1973	1975	1993	2016
Six countries (France, West Germany, Italy, Belgium, the Netherlands and Luxembourg) join their steel and coal industries together, forming the ECSC. These countries also agree never to build up armed forces on their own, and without the others knowing	The ECSC group is renamed the EEC. Member countries further agree to cooperate with each other in producing nuclear power	The EEC begins to trade with other countries as a single group, to form the biggest trading organisation in the world	Britain, Denmark and Ireland are admitted into the EEC	A UK **referendum** is held to decide whether Britain should remain part of the EEC. The result is two to one in favour of staying in	The EEC becomes the European Union (EU)	A UK referendum is held again. The result is 52 per cent to 48 per cent to leave the EU. The UK leaves the EU in 2020

few applications to join the EEC were blocked by France, as the French were suspicious of Britain's relationship with the USA, and of its trade links with Commonwealth countries.

The impact of the Cold War

At the same time, the USA and the USSR became the world's superpowers after the world wars. They became rivals and each tried to prevent the other from gaining too much power. This period of tension was known as the Cold War. Other countries also supported the rivalry: for example, the USA built a close relationship with Britain, while the USSR forged strong links with countries in Eastern Europe such as Hungary and Poland.

In the meantime, Britain was finally admitted into the EEC in 1973; Denmark and Ireland joined on the same day. And in 1979, the European parliament was created and **MEPs** (Members of the European Parliament) were elected by EEC citizens. At first, the European parliament could just advise, but now it can pass laws that apply to all member countries. In the 1980s, three more countries joined the EEC, and a **single market** was proposed. This meant that goods, services and people could move freely between all 12 EEC countries.

In the early 1990s, the Maastricht Treaty was signed, the EEC became the **European Union (EU)**, and a single market was formalised. All countries agreed to extend cooperation even further to include foreign affairs. Another three countries became members, and the EU agreed to accept more members in the future.

The early 1990s also marked the end of the Cold War, when the USSR's influence and control over many countries in Eastern Europe stopped. Many of these newly independent nations wanted to join the EU – eight joined in 2004 (along with Cyprus and Malta), followed by Romania and Bulgaria in 2007, and Croatia in 2013. This brought the total number of EU member countries to 28.

In 1999, 12 member countries agreed to adopt the Euro as their currency. Soon, around 300 million Europeans were carrying the same coins and notes in their pockets. However, Britain did not adopt the Euro, which is now used in 19 of the 28 member countries.

A divided Britain

The British public was divided over its EU membership since it joined. Those in favour of Britain remaining a part of the EU believed that the country benefited

from the strong trade links and 'collective security' of its membership. These people were known as **pro-Europeans**. However, those against it argued that Britain is different from other European countries. They felt that Britain's unique history, traditions and culture should be preserved and not changed in any way to 'fit in' with the rest of the EU. They worried that Britain had lost its independence and identity, and should be free to make its own decisions. These people were called **Eurosceptics**. In 2016, people in the UK voted to leave the EU (in a process that became known as 'Brexit', meaning 'British Exit'). The UK eventually left the EU in 2020.

▼ **A** *The evolution of the European Union, showing membership by decade*

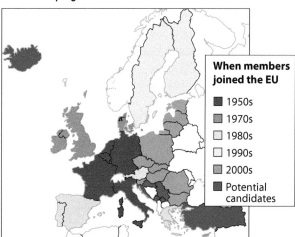

When members joined the EU
- 1950s
- 1970s
- 1980s
- 1990s
- 2000s
- Potential candidates

Work

1 Explain why many European countries wanted to increase cooperation between themselves in the 1950s.

2 Why did Britain decide not to join in the beginning?

3 Why do you think Britain eventually joined?

4 How did the Cold War affect the EU?

5 What different beliefs are held by pro-Europeans and Eurosceptics?

12.2 Migration in Europe

Being a part of the European Union (EU) means there is free movement of workers – this means EU citizens can work in any other EU member state on the same conditions as the citizens of that state. As a result, every year, numerous Europeans move between European countries. Europe is also a popular destination for people who do not live in the EU: with non-EU citizens, individual countries can decide how many they will admit. What has been the impact of migration over the years? Why and how have migration figures changed? And what do we mean by the term 'net migration'?

Objectives

▶ **Define** the different policies relating to EU and non-EU migration.

▶ **Examine** statistics relating to EU and non-EU migration into Britain.

▶ **Assess** how migration has affected Britain and Europe.

Migration within the EU

There is a huge amount of migration within the EU. After 47 years, the UK left the EU in 2020. As a result, the UK is not subject to the same rules as other EU nations in relation to migration. However, for many years other EU citizens could freely come and work in the UK. In the 1970s, for example, around 20,000 EU citizens entered Britain every year, rising to about 60,000 per year by the early 2000s. There was a huge increase in immigration into Britain from EU countries in 2004 when ten more countries joined the EU, including Eastern European nations such as Poland, Hungary and the Czech Republic. These countries were generally poorer than many of the existing EU countries, so the wealthier countries such as Britain, Germany and France attracted people from the new EU countries. Between 2004 and 2006, around 600,000 Eastern European immigrants came to Britain, mostly looking for work and better pay. Many found jobs in construction and retail, often earning five times as much as they did in their home countries.

Fact

Britain operates a points-based system for EU immigrants wanting to work in the UK. Applicants are awarded points depending on their skills, education, income and age. Top priority is given to those with the highest skills and the greatest talents: scientists, engineers, academics and other highly skilled workers.

What were the impacts of migration?

When the EU was expanded in 2004, the largest group of new EU migrants into Britain were from Poland. Using Poland as an example, table **A** outlines the impacts of this migration on both Britain and Poland.

▼ **A** *The impacts of Polish immigration to Britain on both Britain and Poland*

Impacts on Britain (the host country)	Impacts on Poland (the source country)
Many immigrants are young, hardworking and motivated. Many fill job shortages in farm work, building and healthcare. Local services such as schools and housing can sometimes be strained in some communities. Local and national economy benefits because of the immigrants renting houses, buying goods and services, and paying taxes.	Money sent back to Poland helps the Polish economy. There are fewer unemployed people in Poland. There are fewer skilled workers in Poland (such as dentists and plumbers). Poland's population is ageing because so many younger workers are leaving. This also means the Polish government does not receive tax from these people.

Migration from outside the EU

After the Second World War, immigration was encouraged by the British government. Immigrants came mainly from current or former countries of the British Empire. Britain tightened immigration controls in the 1970s, but many thousands of non-EU migrants still come to Britain.

Britain also operates a points-based system for non-EU immigrants. Applicants are awarded points depending on their skills, education, income and age. If an applicant reaches a certain total of points, then they are given a **visa** to allow them entry into Britain for work, especially if there is a shortage of labour in that sector. Britain also gives permission for thousands of non-EU citizens to come into the country to study at colleges and universities. Some of the most common non-EU countries where immigrants come into Britain from are India, Pakistan, the Philippines, Australia, China, the USA and Bangladesh.

What is net migration?

Before 2020, there were roughly the same number of EU citizens moving into Britain as there were non-EU citizens. But people also leave Britain too. People emigrate for all sorts of reasons – including a better job, a better climate or more opportunities.

Net migration is the final change in population after all the people leaving Britain (emigrating) and all the people moving into Britain (immigrating) have been taken into account. Graph **B** below shows Britain's net migration figures from 2005 to 2015. The figures clearly fluctuate a lot, but overall, net migration has remained roughly the same.

People have different opinions about the impact of migration on Britain. Some believe that immigration damages community relations, and that there is great public anxiety over issues such as pressure on public services. Others argue that most immigrants are young and able, so they work and pay more in taxes, use less of the public healthcare and education services, and help with the economic growth of the country.

Key Words

host country   source country   visa
net migration

Fact

In recent years, there has been a growing number of refugees looking to enter the EU from war-torn countries like Afghanistan, Iraq and Syria. Many governments (including in Britain) have restricted refugee access but the EU is working on a new long-term approach to migration for asylum seekers.

Extension

Poland and Britain have a long tradition of friendship going back to the start of the Second World War. Research the links between Poland and Britain, and Polish communities in Britain since the Second World War.

Practice Question

Have governments been the main factor in population movements in the twentieth century?

16 marks

SPaG: 4 marks

Study Tip

In your answer consider the influence of government and other factors such as the desire for a better standard of living.

▼ **B** *Immigration to and emigration from Britain, 2005–15*

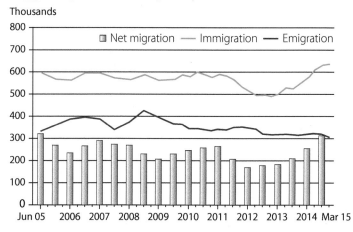

Thousands

Work

1   What is meant by the term 'free movement of workers'?

2   Why did immigration to Britain increase after 2004?

3   In what ways can immigration affect: the host country; the source country?

4   Look at graph **B**. What does it show?

How to... analyse significance

In your exam, you will have to deal with a question about the significance of something, such as an event, an issue or a person.

Practice Question

Explain the significance of Cecil Rhodes in relation to the British Empire. **8 marks**

Study Tip

Judging the significance of a person is about looking at the impact that the person had *at the time*, how they affected people *in the long term*, and whether they are still *relevant today*.

Over to you

When we say an event, idea or person is significant, we mean more than just that it is important. Judging the significance of an event, idea or person is about looking at the impact that it had at the time and how it affected people, and whether it had long-lasting effects or caused important change. You should also consider whether the event, idea or person is still relevant to the present day. Now, work through the following questions.

1 Start by planning out your response: what do you know about Cecil Rhodes? Try to make notes about what Cecil Rhodes' did *at the time*.

2 Consider Rhodes' role in the British Empire and his *impact during his lifetime*. Write about his thoughts and theories – and also his actions in relation to the British Empire.

3 After you have written about Rhodes' impact at the time, move on to consider how he might have made an impact *in the long term*.

4 Lastly, does Rhodes affect our world *today*? Is his impact still recognised, remembered or debated? Does he still cause controversy perhaps, as he did in his lifetime? Remember that the significance of an event, idea or person can change over time.

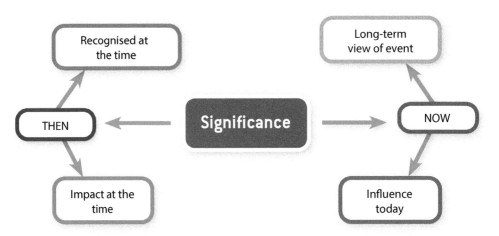

5 Read the following response. Can you identify where the answer explains about Cecil Rhodes being recognised at the time, his immediate impact as well as his long-term impact, and his relevance today?

Cecil Rhodes was significant for his achievements. He made an enormous amount of money from diamonds and later gold and his De Beers diamond company is still important today. Scholarships to university are still paid for by money from his estate. He was responsible for establishing British influence in the southern half of Africa. He established a private empire in Southern and Northern Rhodesia, countries that were named after him. However, he never achieved his imperialist ambition to link the north and south of Africa, from Cairo to the Cape. Nevertheless he was inspired by harmful imperialist ideas that the English race was superior and destined to rule. He thought that it was right to use military force for this aim. Today Rhodes is significant because he is seen by many people to represent everything that was bad about the British Empire in Africa — its arrogance and greed. At the time Cecil Rhodes was significant because he made sure that Britain did well out of the 'scramble for Africa'.

6 Now try to answer the Practice Question on page 100 yourself!

How to... analyse sources

In your exam, you will have to deal with a question about the usefulness of a source to a historian studying that particular part of history. You will be asked a question that directly relates to a source.

▼ **SOURCE A** *A painting by Scottish artist Thomas Faed, called* The Last of the Clan, *painted in 1865. The painting focuses on people who are left behind (those too old or too young to leave) as Scots emigrate to foreign countries during the time of the Highland Clearances. The viewer's vantage point is the deck of a departing ship, looking at the last images an emigrating Scot might ever have of his homeland and his clan.*

Practice Question

Study **Source A**. How useful is **Source A** to a historian studying Scottish emigration from the Highlands in the eighteenth and nineteenth centuries?

8 marks

Study Tip

Ask yourself, 'What is this source?' In this case it is a painting. The provenance (such as the date of publication, the type of source, and the title) will help you to assess the usefulness of the source. What do you know about the topic that you can link with the information from the provenance?

Study Tip

With all visual sources, try to think of three Cs:

Context: what was going on at the time the source was created?

Content: what does the source show? What is happening? What can you see?

Comment: what point is the artist trying to make about the events portrayed?

The usefulness of a source is what it tells you about the history of the time. A source might be useful because it reveals something new, why events turned out the way they did, or why people acted or thought in a particular way at that time. This question suggests that the source has a use: remember this as you work through the following questions.

1 Start by analysing the content of **Source A**. What is the author trying to say about the Highland Clearances? And what does it tell us about the topic that makes it useful or not? The content of the source should be checked against your own knowledge of the topic.

2 You should also consider the provenance of **Source A**:

a What does it tell you about how useful, or not, the source might be? Provenance could mean who produced the source, why it was produced, who it was produced for, where and when it was produced.

b What was the context of the time in which the source was created? Remember that to answer a question about the usefulness of a source, the provenance of a source is just as important as the content.

3 Recall the actual question: it asks about a historian studying the Highland Clearances. In **Source A**, the artist has painted a number of different things in the scene. Do you think he is trying to make you feel a particular way about the clearances? Why might this be?

4 Now try to finish this answer! You could use some of these sentence starters to help you compose your answer.

> The source is useful because it comes from the time of the Highland Clearances, so it shows what some people (in this case, the artist) were thinking about the clearances. The painting shows...
>
> The artist is trying to get the viewer of his painting to...
>
> I know from my own knowledge that...
>
> However, despite this painting being useful, it is one man's view or interpretation of the clearances so...

5 Now try to answer the Practice Question on page 100 yourself!

How to... compare similarities

In your exam, you will have to deal with a question about comparing the similarities of two things, such as two events or developments.

Practice Question

Explain two ways in which Huguenot migration to Britain and Irish migration to Britain were similar.   **8 marks**

Study Tip

With this type of question, it is important to think about the *similarities* between the two topics or aspects of history you have studied, and not the *differences*.

Over to you

This style of question asks you to explain the similarities between two topics or aspects of the history you have studied. You are looking for similarities between the two events: remember this as you work through the following questions.

1   Start by planning out your response: what are the similarities between Huguenot migration to Britain and Irish migration to Britain? Make a list or a mind-map to help you analyse the similarities. For example, when explaining the two events, consider:

   a   causes: why did the event happen?

   b   development: how did the event develop?

   c   consequences: events will have results.

2   Try to organise your response in three sections, covering causes, development and consequences. Remember that you will need to show how well you have understood both events by explaining the similarities that you can find.

3   Read the following response. Can you identify where the answer explains about similarities in terms of causes, development and consequences?

> There are a number of similarities between both the Huguenot migration to Britain and Irish migration to Britain. For example, both the Huguenots and the Irish left their own countries because they felt that they could no longer lead the sorts of lives they wanted. Both groups of people were pushed out of the place where they were living. The Huguenots were pushed out because of persecution for their religion after the Edict of Nantes was withdrawn in 1685. The Irish were pushed out because of hunger caused by the potato famine and the failure of the potato crop in the mid-nineteenth century. Although many French Huguenots and the Irish both found work and a new life in North America, they are similar in that both groups came to Britain. The Irish found work in the factories of the big cities, and the Huguenots used their weaving and silk skills in the textile industry.

4   Now try to answer the Practice Question yourself!

How to... evaluate main factors

In your exam, you will have to deal with a question that asks you to evaluate factors.

Practice Question

Were the two world wars the main factors in causing Britain to lose much of its empire in the twentieth century?

Explain your answer with reference to the two world wars and other factors.

16 marks

SPaG: 4 marks

Study Tip

During your study of migration, empires and the people, you may have noticed a number of factors appearing time and time again. These factors are important because historians not only just describe events that happened in the past, they also explain why they happened. These factors are the causes that have made things happen during your thematic study. This question suggests that war might be the main factor.

Over to you

Different factors have affected your migration, empires and the people thematic study over a long period of time. Those factors are war, religion, government, economic resources, science and technology, ideas such as imperialism, social Darwinism and civilisation, and the role of individuals. Frequently, factors worked together to bring about particular developments at particular times. This question is asking about one particular factor and its influence compared with other factors: remember this as you work through the following questions.

1   Start by writing about the factor that has been named in the question: in this case, it is about the two world wars. Think carefully about these two wars and recall how they might have contributed to the decline of the British Empire in the twentieth century. The factor you are addressing might sometimes have *helped* and sometimes *hindered* the development of the British Empire – make sure you make a note of this.

2   Next, consider other factors that have influenced the break-up of the British Empire in the twentieth century. Choose two or three other factors from your study and explain, with examples, how those factors might have contributed to the decline of the British Empire.

3   Lastly, you will have to deal with the *judgement* in the question. The question picked out that war was the main factor. You have to say whether or not you agree with this. Try to weigh up or assess the factor of war against any other factors you have mentioned, and say which was more important. To back up your conclusion, you should also explain *why*, with supporting evidence.

4   Read the following essay conclusion to the question. Can you identify: the given factor (the two world wars) and two other factors? The supporting points about each factor? An assessment or judgement about which is the main factor?

> The twentieth-century world wars were a factor that exhausted Britain financially and militarily. When Britain gained its colonies, military power had been used to establish control. After 1945, when Britain's 'authority' was challenged, there was no longer any military power to back it up. And the empire was too big and Britain too poor to do anything about it. But Britain's authority was challenged by nationalist independence movements in the empire. These powerful, committed movements convinced both world opinion and the British government to loosen its grip on its colonies in the latter half of the twentieth century. I think this was the main factor.

5   Now try to answer the Practice Question on page 100 yourself!

Practice Questions for Paper 2: Britain: Migration, empires and the people: c790 to the present day

The examination questions on the Migration, Empires and the People c790–Present Day thematic study will be varied but there will be a question on a source (AO3), a question on significance (AO1 and AO2), a similarity/difference question (AO1 and AO2), and an extended writing question using factors (AO1 and AO2). Below is a selection of these different kinds of questions for you to practise.

Answer **all four** questions. You are advised to spend 50 minutes on these four questions.

Source A   A seventeenth-century drawing of Captain John Smith's encounter with indigenous people in Virginia; Smith was a well-known early British settler who became internationally famous when Disney animated the story of Pocahontas. The drawing appeared in a book published in 1624 by Captain Smith, called *The Generall Historie of Virginia, New-England, and the Summer Isles*.

1   Study **Source A**.

    How useful is **Source A** to a historian studying the impact on the indigenous peoples of the
    British colonisation of North America?

    Explain your answer using **Source A** and your contextual knowledge.   `8 marks`

2   Explain the significance of the Hundred Years' War.   `8 marks`

3   Explain two ways in which England's loss of European land in Medieval times and the loss of the British Empire in
    the twentieth century were similar.   `8 marks`

4   Has the economic factor been the main cause of people migrating **from and within** Britain?

    Explain your answer with reference to the economic factor and other factors.

    Use examples from your study of Migration, empires and the people.   `16 marks`
    `SPaG: 4 marks`

Glossary

13 colonies 13 British colonies in America that would eventually become the United States of America

Aboriginal people people who inhabit land before the arrival of colonists

Anglican relating to the Church of England or any of the Churches related to it in origin

asylum protection given by a country to someone who has left their home country

baron man who had been given high rank by the king; the title came with land

Boer South African person of Dutch descent

Boston Tea Party violent demonstration in 1773 by American colonists prior to the American War of Independence

Catholic Christian who follows the teachings of the Catholic Church

chain migration process by which immigrants follow family member to a new place; often, laws allow immigrants to reunite with family in the new destination

civil war war between different groups in one country

colonise send settlers to a place and establish control over it

colour bar segregation of people based on colour or race, especially any barrier to black people participating in activities

commodity goods that are traded for other goods; this might be food, produce or even enslaved people

Commonwealth voluntary association of independent nations and dependent territories linked by historical ties (as parts of the former British Empire) and cooperating on matters of mutual concern, especially regarding economics and trade

constitution written document stating how a country or state is to be governed

crusade religious war fought in the Middle Ages between Christians and Muslims

Danegeld land tax levied in Anglo-Saxon England to raise funds for protection against Danish invaders

Danelaw part of northern and eastern England occupied and controlled by Danes from the late ninth century until after the Norman Conquest

democratic system of government where people elect their representatives; belief in social equality

diaspora group of people from a small geographical area scattered across different countries

dominion semi-independent country that was part of the British Empire but had its own government

Edict of Nantes agreement granting Protestants civil rights in France in 1598; revoked in 1685 by Louis XIV of France

emigrants people who move out of a country

empire collection of communities, regions, territories, states or countries that are ruled over and controlled by one leader or 'mother country'; the areas controlled are usually called colonies (although sometimes dominions or dependencies); the mother country makes many of the key decisions to do with the places it rules over

enslaved made a slave; having one's freedom to choose or act taken away

European Coal and Steel Community (ECSC) group of six countries (France, West Germany, Italy, Belgium, the Netherlands and Luxembourg) that joined together their steel and coal industries in 1951

European Economic Community (EEC) new name for the ECSC, created in 1957; the group also agreed to cooperate with each other in producing nuclear power

European Union (EU) group of European countries that participates in the world economy as one economic unit

Eurosceptic person opposed to Britain's role in the EU

exclusion zone area into which entry is forbidden, especially by ships or aircraft from particular nations

forced migration when migrants move because they have no choice and are forced to

guerrilla member of a small group of soldiers who do not belong to a regular army; they usually fight as independent units and wage small-scale attacks on their enemies

heretic non-believer, or believer in an opposing religion

Highland Clearances forced eviction during the eighteenth and nineteenth centuries of a large number of people from land they farmed in the Scottish Highlands

host country country that takes in immigrants

hunter-gather person who lives by gathering food, like nuts and berries, and kills wild animals for meat and fur

immigrants people who move into a country

imperial propaganda a government's attempts to spread a set of ideas and beliefs about empire and conquest

imperialist person who practises or supports imperialism, which is a set of ideas and beliefs about empire and conquest

indenture system labour system in which people paid for their passage to a new country by working for an employer for a fixed term of years

indentured servant person who paid for their passage to a new country by signing a contract stating that they would work for a set period of time; indentured servitude was usually voluntary but was sometimes used as a form of punishment

Indian National Congress political organisation that led the campaign for Indian independence

indigenous American (also known as Native American) person that is a member of any of the first groups of people living in North and South America or the Caribbean

infantry soldiers who fight on foot

internal migration refers to people within a country moving to another location within its borders

Jacobite Rebellions rebellions in the 1700s that aimed to help the Stuarts regain the British throne; 'Jacobus' is Latin for James, the first Stuart king of England

Jamestown early British colony established in the name of King James I

jingoism feeling or belief that a person's country is always right; jingoism means being in favour of aggressive acts against other countries

Kenya African Union political group that campaigned for both independence for Kenya and access to white-owned land

Magna Carta document written in 1215 that recognised people's rights to certain basic liberties

Maroons a group of formerly enslaved people (and their descendants) who gained their freedom by escaping the plantations to live in a remote location

Mau Mau Rebellion military conflict that took place in British Kenya, between 1952 and 1960, between groups that wanted Kenya to become an independent nation and British forces who wished Kenya to remain part of the British Empire

MEP Member of the European Parliament

migrant person who moves from one place to another

monopoly complete control of the entire supply of goods or of a service in a certain area

Muslim League political party established in the British Indian Empire; it worked for the establishment of a separate Muslim-majority nation-state, Pakistan

mutineer person who takes part in an open rebellion against authority

National Congress of British West Africa organisation that campaigned to the British government for West Africans to have more control of their own affairs

nationalism having strong patriotic feelings, especially a belief in the superiority of one's own country over others

Navigation Acts series of laws that restricted the use of foreign ships for trade between every country except Britain

navvy labourer employed in building a road or railway

net migration final change in population after all the people leaving a country (emigrating) and all the people moving into a country (immigrating) have been taken into account

New World name for the territories that Europeans first reached, from the 1400s, such as the Americas

partition division of British India into separate independent countries

persecution when someone or a group of people are abused or punished, often for their beliefs

Pilgrim Fathers group of 102 people, led by English Puritans fleeing religious persecution, who sailed to the 'new world' of America and founded a new colony in 1620

piracy when sailors steal cargoes from other ships, or even the ships themselves

plantation large farm that specialises in growing usually just one crop

plunder to steal from a place or person, usually using force

pogrom large-scale, targeted and repeated persecution of an ethnic or religious group, particularly Jews

privateer private sea captain given permission to raid and capture enemy ships

pro-European person in favour of Britain's place in the EU

Protestant member of Christian group that protested against the Catholic Church; there are many types or denominations of Protestants, including Quakers and Puritans

Puritan hard-line Protestant Christian who believes in simple church services and lifestyles; Puritans protested against the practices of the Catholic Church

Quaker member of Protestant Christian group, also known as the Religious Society of Friends, that believes in equality between members

referendum vote in which all the people eligible to vote in a country or area are asked to give their opinion of or decide on an important political or social issue

Reformation the 'break with Rome' by Henry VIII in 1534, when he made England's official religion Protestantism rather than Catholicism

refugee person who has been forced to leave their country in order to escape war, persecution or natural disaster

republic country with a system of government where an elected President has supreme power, rather than a monarch

Royal African Company monopoly (the only company allowed to invest) in slavery run from Britain in the 1600s

rural relating to the countryside, rather than a town or city

scorched earth military strategy that involves destroying anything that might be useful to the enemy while advancing through or withdrawing from an area

Sepoy an Indian soldier serving with the British Army or another European power

single market shared agreement that means that goods, services, money and people can move freely between EU member countries

slave triangle three-part trading journey in which traders traded goods for enslaved people in Africa; enslaved people for different goods in the Americas; and these goods for money in Britain

social Darwinism based on Darwin's theory of evolution, which said that weaker animals would die out and stronger ones would evolve and survive. This theory was applied to countries or peoples, and made people like Cecil Rhodes think it was right for those they perceived as stronger, such as Britain, to take over weaker countries

source country country where immigrants have travelled from

Stamp Act act that imposed a tax on printed materials (such as legal documents, magazines, playing cards and newspapers) paid to Britain and used in the colonies of British America

task force part of a country's armed forces that is given the job of working on a single defined task or activity

trading station large warehouse at a port where goods were stored and where trading took place

transportation the sending of convicted criminals to a penal colony

tribe a social group made up of families or communities linked by social, economic or religious similarities, often with a common culture and language

Ulster Plantations provinces or areas in the north of Ireland that were colonised by settlers from England and Scotland

urban relating to a town or city

urbanisation process by which large numbers of people move to urban areas, creating larger towns and cities

viceroy someone who rules a country, province or colony on behalf of a sovereign; for example, in the 1850s a viceroy was put in charge of India on behalf of Queen Victoria

Viking Scandinavian pirates and traders who raided and settled in many parts of northern Europe in the eighth to the eleventh centuries

Virginia Britain's first colony, set up under time of Elizabeth I (the 'Virgin Queen'), and so named after her

visa authorised document that allows a person to enter a country

voluntary migration when migrants move because they choose to leave a particular place of their own free will, rather than being forced to

Witan national council or parliament in Anglo-Saxon England

Index

Acknowledgements

The publisher and authors would like to thank the following for permission to use photographs and other copyright material:

Cover: FPG/Staff/Getty Images.

Photos: **p6(l)**: Look and Learn; **p6(m)**: Mary Evans Picture Library; **p6(r)**: Granger Historical Picture Archive / Alamy Stock Photo; **p7(bl)**: FALKENSTEINFOTO/Alamy Stock Photo; **p7(t)**: Daily Herald Archive/Contributor/Getty Images; **p7(br)**: Bettmann/Getty Images; **p8**: The National Trust Photolibrary/Alamy Stock Photo; **p9**: Look and Learn; **p11**: Paul Cummings/Shutterstock; **p12**: Mary Evans Picture Library; **p14**: English School, (14th century)/English/British Library Board. All Rights Reserved/Bridgeman Images; **p15**: English School, (11th century)/English/British Library Board. All Rights Reserved/Bridgeman Images; **p16**: English School, (14th century)/English/British Library Board. All Rights Reserved/Bridgeman Images; **p18**: World History Archive/Alamy Stock Photo; **p20**: GL Archive/Alamy Stock Photo; **p22**: Lebrecht Music and Arts Photo Library/Alamy Stock Photo; **p24**: Mary Evans Picture Library; **p26(t)**: Mary Evans Picture Library; **p29**: Mary Evans Picture Library; **p30**: DEA/G. DAGLI ORTI/De Agostini/Getty Images; **p33**: Niday Picture Library/Alamy Stock Photo; **p35**: GL Archive/Alamy Stock Photo; **p36**: American School, (19th century)/American/Bridgeman Images; **p37**: Duncan1890/iStockphoto; **p39**: American School, (18th century)/American/Bridgeman Images; **p40**: Granger Historical Picture Archive/Alamy Stock Photo; **p42**: Mary Evans Picture Library; **p43**: Chronicle/Alamy Stock Photo; **p45**: Faed, Thomas (1826-1900)/Scottish/Bridgeman Images; **p46**: Mary Evans Picture Library; **p48**: Mary Evans/Pharcide; **p50**: Lloyd, W. (19th century)/English/Bridgeman Images; **p51**: Davie, Howard (fl.1914-44)/English/Bridgeman Images; **p52**: FALKENSTEINFOTO/Alamy Stock Photo; **p54**: Illustrated London News Ltd/Mary Evans; **p55**: Christophe Boisvieux/The Image Bank/Getty Images; **p57**: The Print Collector/Alamy Stock Photo; **p59**: Chronicle/Alamy Stock Photo; **p60**: RODGER BOSCH/Stringer/Getty Images; **p61**: Stock Montage, Inc./Alamy Stock Photo; **p62**: Mary Evans/Grenville Collins Postcard Collection; **p63**: Pictorial Press Ltd/Alamy Stock Photo; **p65**: Hulton-Deutsch Collection/CORBIS/Getty Images; **p66**: Mary Evans Picture Library; **p68**: Corbis Historical/Getty Images; **p69**: Mary Evans Picture Library; **p70**: Pictorial Press Ltd/Alamy Stock Photo; **p72**: Mary Evans Picture Library; **p73**: Culture Club/Getty Images; **p74**: Mary Evans / Sueddeutsche Zeitung Photo; **p75**: Florilegius / Mary Evans; **p79**: Mary Evans / SZ Photo / Scherl; **p80**: Bettmann/Getty Images; **p81**: Hulton-Deutsch Collection/Corbis Historical/Getty Images; **p84(l)**: Daily Herald Archive/Contributor/Getty Images; **p84(r)**: Courtesy of the Cross family; **p85**: Meager/Stringer/Getty Images; **p86(tr)**: Popperfoto/Contributor/Getty Images; **p86(ml)**: Charles Hewitt/Picture Post/Hulton Archive/Getty Images; **p87**: FPG/Archive Photos/Getty Images; **p88**: Bettmann/Getty Images; **p96**: Faed, Thomas (1826-1900)/Scottish/Bridgeman Images; **p100**: Duncan1890/iStockphoto.

Artwork by Q2A Media Services Pvt. Ltd.

We are grateful to the authors and publishers for use of extracts from their titles and in particular to the following:

AQA for practice questions from the AQA GCSE History Paper 2 'Shaping the Nation', copyright © 2015 AQA and its licensors. AQA accepts no responsibility for the study tips given which have neither been provided nor approved by AQA.

Guardian News and Media Ltd for 'Cecil Rhodes colonial legacy must fall - not his statue' by Siya Mnyanda, *The Guardian*, 25 March 2015, copyright © Guardian News and Media Ltd 2015, 2021.

Hodder Education for *The British Empire, 1815-1914* by Frank McDonough (Hodder, 1994).

United Agents (www.unitedagents.co.uk) on behalf of the author's estate for *Pax Britannica* by Jan Morris (Faber, 1968), copyright © James Morris 1968.

Every effort has been made to contact copyright holders of material reproduced in this book. Any omissions will be rectified in subsequent printings if notice is given to the publisher.

Topics available from *Oxford AQA GCSE History*

Germany 1890–1945: Democracy and Dictatorship
Student Book
978 019 837010 9
Kerboodle Book
978 019 837014 7

America 1920–1973: Opportunity and Inequality
Student Book
978 019 841262 5
Kerboodle Book
978 019 841263 2

Conflict and Tension First World War 1894–1918
Student Book
978 019 842900 5
Kerboodle Book
978 019 842901 2

Conflict and Tension: The Inter-War Years 1918–1939
Student Book
978 019 837011 6
Kerboodle Book
978 019 837015 4

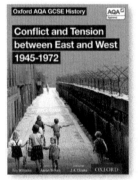

Conflict and Tension between East and West 1945–1972
Student Book
978 019 841266 3
Kerboodle Book
978 019 841267 0

Conflict and Tension in Asia 1950–1975
Student Book
978 019 841264 9
Kerboodle Book
978 019 841265 6

Health and the People c1000–Present Day
Student Book
978 138 202310 8
Kerboodle Book
978 138 202312 2

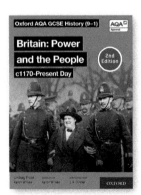

Power and the People c1170–Present Day
Student Book
978 138 202313 9
Kerboodle Book
978 138 202315 3

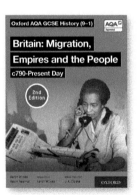

Migration, Empires and the People c790–Present Day
Student Book
978 138 202307 8
Kerboodle Book
978 138 202309 2

British Depth Studies c1066–1685
Student Book
978 019 837012 3
Kerboodle Book
978 019 837016 1

Time-saving expert support for all 16 AQA options

Teacher Handbook
978 019 837018 5

Professional, practical support filled with subject knowledge, classroom ideas and activities, plus exam advice and support.

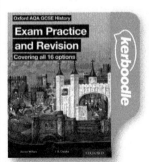

Kerboodle Exam Practice and Revision
978 019 837019 2

An online resource packed full of exam practice, revision and continuing timesaving support for the entire specification.

 **RECAP**  **APPLY**  **REVIEW** ✓ **SUCCEED**

**Germany 1890–1945
Revision Guide**
978 019 842289 1

**America 1920–1973:
Opportunity and Inequality
Revision Guide**
978 019 843282 1

Oxford AQA GCSE History (9-1)
**Conflict and Tension:
First World War
1894-1918
Revision Guide**

**Conflict and Tension
First World War 1894–1918
Revision Guide**
978 138 200767 2

**Give
students the
confidence
to succeed**

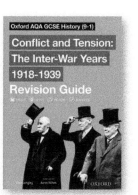

**Conflict and Tension:
The Inter-War Years 1918–1939
Revision Guide**
978 019 842291 4

Oxford AQA GCSE History (9-1)
**Conflict and Tension
between East and West
1945-1972
Revision Guide**

**Conflict and Tension
between East and West
1945–1972 Revision Guide**
978 019 843288 3

**Conflict and Tension in Asia
1950–1975 Revision Guide**
978 019 843286 9

Oxford AQA GCSE History (9-1)
**Britain: Health and the
People c1000-Present Day
Revision Guide**

**Britain: Health and the
People c1000–Present
Day Revision Guide**
978 019 842295 2

**Britain: Power and the
People c1170–Present
Day Revision Guide**
978 019 843290 6

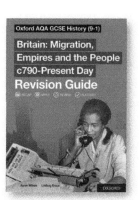

**Britain: Migration, Empires
and the People c790–Present
Day Revision Guide**
978 138 201503 5

Oxford AQA GCSE History (9-1)
**Norman England
c1066-c1100
Revision Guide**

**Norman England
c1066–c.1100 Revision Guide**
978 019 843284 5

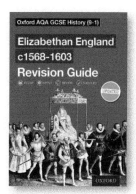

**Elizabethan England
c1568–1603 Revision Guide**
978 019 842293 8

All published Student Books have been approved by AQA. The Kerboodle: Exam Practice and Revision, Teacher Handbook, and Revision Guides have not been approved by AQA.

Order online at **www.oxfordsecondary.com/gcsehistory**